7/8/17

Tyress:

Thank you for your support. May God continue to Bless you as you RENEW your life!

Kenneth Hollingshed
Hannah Hollingshed

1/8/17

Jess,

Thank you so much for going the extra mile as my editor for Law Review.

Your friend,
Jamie Kingston

40 DAY
FINANCIAL RENEWAL

Tanesha and Kenneth Hollingshed

WESTBOW
PRESS
A DIVISION OF THOMAS NELSON
& ZONDERVAN

Copyright © 2017 Tanesha and Kenneth Hollingshed.

All rights reserved. No part of this book may be used or reproduced by any means, graphic, electronic, or mechanical, including photocopying, recording, taping or by any information storage retrieval system without the written permission of the author except in the case of brief quotations embodied in critical articles and reviews.

WestBow Press books may be ordered through booksellers or by contacting:

WestBow Press
A Division of Thomas Nelson & Zondervan
1663 Liberty Drive
Bloomington, IN 47403
www.westbowpress.com
1 (866) 928-1240

Because of the dynamic nature of the Internet, any web addresses or links contained in this book may have changed since publication and may no longer be valid. The views expressed in this work are solely those of the author and do not necessarily reflect the views of the publisher, and the publisher hereby disclaims any responsibility for them.

Any people depicted in stock imagery provided by Thinkstock are models, and such images are being used for illustrative purposes only. Certain stock imagery © Thinkstock.

Scripture quotations are taken from the Holy Bible, New International Version®, NIV®. Copyright © 1973, 1978, 1984, 2011 by Biblica, Inc.™ Used by permission of Zondervan. All rights reserved worldwide.

ISBN: 978-1-5127-8373-5 (sc)
ISBN: 978-1-5127-8374-2 (hc)
ISBN: 978-1-5127-8372-8 (e)

Library of Congress Control Number: 2017905622

Print information available on the last page.

WestBow Press rev. date: 4/24/2017

DEDICATION

We dedicate this book to our boys, Khaylen and Kingston.

To Khaylen and Kingston: We pray that you have learned from our struggles. We hope that everything that we have taught you about God and your personal finances will resonate with you for the rest of your lives. Make good financial choices so that you can build wealth and pass it down to the next generation. We love you both dearly.

In loving memory of our beautiful daughter, Kennedi Iman Hollingshed (deceased). She was born on June 3, 2003, and transitioned to her heavenly home on May 5, 2005. There is not a day that goes by that we do not think about her. We treasure the memories of life with us. Kennedi taught us so much without being able say a word. She taught us resilience, patience, how to cope with the unexpected, how to care for children with special needs, and how to build character. We love and miss her so much.

Love,
Dad and Mom

ACKNOWLEDGMENT

To the North Park CME Church Family:

We thank you for being the first to experience the Forty-Day Financial Renewal with us. Some of you walked with us through the entire forty days. We thank you for the wonderful testimonies. We pray that those of you who did not participate will try it and watch what God will do with your spiritual life and finances. You too will have a testimony. We co-wrote this book specifically with you in mind. We want you to be prosperous because when you are prosperous, it gives you the power to bless God, your church, and others.

    The number 40 usually has to do with testing in the Bible. As you know, we have had many tests right there at North Park CME Church. You have watched us pass many life-altering tests. We thank God for giving us the strength to pass the tests and for your continual prayers. You have so much to gain from this forty-day financial-renewal experience. Your faith will be tested, but we believe you are going to pass the test and experience some major financial breakthroughs and unexpected blessings! We love you all.

Yours because of Him,
Kenneth and Tanesha

SPECIAL THANKS

We thank God for a great team of people who have supported us through our journey of writing, editing, publishing, and marketing this book. A special thanks to our friends: Retired Bishop Ronald Cunningham of the Christian Methodist Episcopal Church and his lovely wife, Lady Clarice Cunningham for taking time to read our manuscript during the editing process and for providing us with positive feedback. Our current bishop, Senior Bishop Lawrence L. Reddick III of the Christian Methodist Episcopal Church and his lovely wife, Wynde Jones Reddick for their leadership, prayers support, and encouragement during the writing and production of our book. Judy with Labels Designer Consignment Boutique in Dallas for blessing me with a beautiful designer suit for our author photo shoot. We thank Tomea Coleman-Lockhart for applying Mocca Makeup and Skincare for my photo shoot. We thank our photographer, Brian Guilliaux for doing such an excellent job on our author photos.

CONTENTS

Introduction xiii
Renewing My Understanding of Money xxxi
SMARTER Goal Worksheet xxxvii

Part I: Renewing My Covenant with God

Day 1   A New Covenant with God 1
Day 2   Under New Management 6
Day 3   First Fruits 10
Day 4   Write the Vision 14
Day 5   Financial Equality 18
Day 6   God's Power to Do More 22
Day 7   Storing Up Treasures 25
Day 8   True Treasures of the Heart 28
Day 9   Serving a Miracle-Working God 31
Day 10   Breaking the Financial Curse 35

Part II: Renewing My Spirit

Day 11   Putting Faith in Action 41
Day 12   It Shall Be Done if You Believe 45
Day 13   Being Content 48
Day 14   Touch and Agree 51
Day 15   Being a Cheerful Giver 55
Day 16   Being a Generous Giver 58
Day 17   Trusting God for a Financial Breakthrough 62

Day 18	Investing Wisely	65
Day 19	Seeking God First	71
Day 20	Prayer for Spiritual Insight	74

Part III: Renewing My Mind

Day 21	Receiving God's Blessings	81
Day 22	Pay It Forward	84
Day 23	Reaping and Sowing	88
Day 24	Living in Financial Peace	92
Day 25	The Great I Am	96
Day 26	Leaving a Legacy	99
Day 27	Jesus Promised He'll Take Care of Me	103
Day 28	My Latter Will Be Greater	109
Day 29	Give Us Our Daily Bread	112
Day 30	Growing in Love	115

Part IV: Renewing My Financial Plan

Day 31	Facing Fears	121
Day 32	Obedience Is Better than Sacrifice	125
Day 33	Sacrifice a Thanks Offering	129
Day 34	A Season of Renewal	132
Day 35	Being Wonderfully Made	135
Day 36	My Grace Is Sufficient	139
Day 37	Living in the Overflow	142
Day 38	Pray Without Ceasing	145
Day 39	An Abundant Life	148
Day 40	Financial Renewal Testimony	152

Renewal in Heaven	157
About the Authors	163
Appendix	167

INTRODUCTION
The significance of forty days in the Bible

The number 40 is a significant number in the Bible. It is listed several times, from the Old Testament to the New Testament. Most of the time, the number 40 deals with judgment or testing faith. In the Old Testament, God destroyed the earth by causing a flood of continued rain for forty days and forty nights (Genesis 7:12). Even though the flood brought complete destruction to all life on earth, it was a new beginning for Noah and his family. They had a great opportunity to reestablish righteousness on earth by living according to God's Word.

After Moses killed the Egyptian, he fled to Midian, where he spent forty years in the desert tending flocks (Acts 7:30). After forty years had passed, an angel appeared to Moses in the flames of a burning bush and sent him to Pharaoh to bring the Israelites out of Egypt. Moses eventually led 600,000 people out of Egypt (Exodus 24:18). God led them through the desert with a pillar of clouds during the day, and a pillar of fire at night as a guide on their journey to the Promised Land (Exodus 24:18).

Jesus was tempted for forty days and forty nights (Matthew 4:2). He entered the wilderness to pray without food to show His dependence on the bread of heaven, the Word of God. But during His time of temptation, Satan tempts Jesus to turn stones into bread. Jesus replies with the words of scripture, "Man shall not live by bread alone, but by every word that proceeds from the mouth of God". (Matthew 4:4) When Jesus resisted all of Satan's attempts to lead Him astray, Satan left Jesus alone. Then the angels of the Lord came and took care of Jesus. (Matthew 4:11)

There were forty days between Jesus's resurrection and ascension (Acts 1:3). Forty days after Jesus rose from the dead, He walked and talked in places where he had once healed, delivered, preached, and loved so many people. Some of the same people witnessed Jesus's restored body as He is ascended to Heaven to sit down at the right hand of God. (Mark 16:19)

When Ken was forty years old and I was thirty years old, we experienced a life-altering and traumatic experience on June 3, 2003, that changed our lives forever. Ken had already served about a year as senior pastor of North Park C.M.E. Church in Dallas, Texas, before we married on September 11, 1999. It had been four years after our marriage, and I was still trying to settle into my new role as "the pastor's wife" and my new found title, "First Lady." Being called the first lady is a traditional title for pastor's wives in predominantly Black Christian churches. Prior to our marriage, my only reference of First Lady was the wife of the president of the United States of America. That title always made me feel uncomfortable because I viewed it as position of high expectation and perfection. I never felt that I could measure up to being called "first lady" because I knew at age twenty-six I had a lot of growing and learning to do in life. I was bound to disappoint and frustrate some church folks.

At that time, our oldest son, Khaylen, was about six years old. I was blessed to have met and married a great Christian man who was willing to accept and raise my son, Khaylen, as his very own son since he was one-year-old. Ken had never had children of his own, so he immediately bonded with Khaylen. He had always dreamt of having a son. He shared with me how he used to attend youth recreation ball games just to witness the joy of fathers playing sports with their sons. He would fantasize about doing the same one day with his son. We were ecstatic and looking forward to having our first child together. We had been trying to conceive for about three years before we finally received the great news that I was pregnant with our first child. I will never forget the day I told Ken that I was pregnant. His eyes lit up like a child on Christmas day. He was so excited that he shouted and cried tears of joy. God had answered our prayer, and we were anticipating growing our family.

I was working as an accountant and business manager for a major radio station in Dallas. Life seemed to be going good for us until we were faced with one of the biggest challenges of our lives. It reminds us of the lyrics of one of our favorite gospel songs, "You Don't Know My Story" (*Life & Favor*) by John P. Kee. The lyrics read, "You don't know the things that I've come through, you cannot imagine the pain, the trials I've had to endure." This song is our personal testimony. It was during my seventh month of pregnancy. For several weeks, I had been feeling dizzy and weak and had this nagging cramp in my lower abdomen. I knew something was wrong, but every time I would mention it to my OBGYN doctor, he would tell me that it was all a normal part of pregnancy.

On the morning of June 3, 2003, I insisted that my doctor allow me to come in for a routine examination to make sure everything was okay with my baby. When I arrived, I explained to my doctor's nurse that I had not been feeling well. She checked my vitals and immediately noticed that my blood pressure was unusually high. I could not help but notice the look of concern on her face as she wrote down my blood pressure numbers in my chart. She asked me to lie down for a few minutes to see if my blood pressure would go down. Then she called in another nurse to check my blood pressure again, and that person looked even more concerned. They both asked me to lie down until my doctor came in. About thirty minutes later, my doctor came in to check on me. I explained that I was not feeling well and that both of my blood pressure readings were extremely high. He assured me that all of my discomforts including my high blood pressure were a normal part of pregnancy and that I was not in danger.

I left my doctor's office and headed to the mall to get a few things off my "Labor and Delivery Hospital Bag Checklist." I knew that it was getting closer to the arrival of our baby, and I had been gradually checking off my list of items to prepare for my upcoming hospital stay. It was shortly after I arrived at the shopping mall when I began to experience an excruciating and sharp pains in my abdomen. The pain was so severe that I couldn't walk. I felt myself getting weaker and weaker, so I immediately called Ken to tell him where I was and what was happening to me. At the time, I thought I was possibly in labor. I eventually blacked out in the middle of our conversation at the cosmetic counter inside of Dillard's department store. I vaguely remember the paramedics talking to me on the way to the hospital.

When I came to, I was in the emergency room where Ken and the ER doctors were standing by my side with tears in their eyes. From the looks on their faces, I knew that we were in trouble. I learned that my placenta had completely detached from our baby, and I had bled internally by the time the ambulance got me to the emergency room for an emergency C-section. I had suffered from a placenta abruption, a condition where the placenta detaches from the inner wall of the uterus. It was so sudden and literally abrupt! The ER doctors explained that I had gone my entire pregnancy with untreated high blood pressure, which contributed to the placenta abruption.

My daughter lost oxygen to the brain and nutrients for several minutes and I almost died on the delivery table. In fact, I stopped breathing and had to be resuscitated. I am blessed to be alive. Our precious baby was in such bad condition that the medical team had already given up on her. They had taken her off of the breathing machine and were waiting patiently for her to take her last breath. On top of that, we had learned that we could never have more children due to my health concerns. We were devastated! I remember lying in the hospital bed, traumatized with a series of unanswered questions: *How could my doctor not have noticed all of the warning signs? Why didn't my doctor do something to prevent this from happening to me? Why did my doctor ignore all of my concerns of not feeling well? Why didn't my doctor admit me in the hospital as soon as the nurses notified him of my high blood pressure reading in his office that morning?* I was angry, frustrated, and confused. I desperately needed answers.

Once the doctors realized that our daughter was fighting to stay alive and was able to breathe on her own, they took her by Care Flite to the nearest Baylor NICCU (newborn and infant critical care unit) where she would stay for about eight weeks. There was so much uncertainty about whether or not Kennedi would survive. Each day that she was alive was a blessing from God. It seemed like she had wires going through every part of her little body. She was on a breathing machine, she was on a feeding tube, and she was on several different types of medicine to help control her uncontrollable seizures.

The only definitive answers that the doctors could give us was that she was severely brain-injured, which meant she would never walk, talk, or eat on her own. We were in shock! It was surreal. At times it felt like we were living in our own wilderness. As hard as it was for us, we continued to pray, attend church, and pay our tithes in the midst of our trials.

All the medical bills that we had accumulated from Kennedi's stay in the NICCU kept racing through our minds, followed by a series of questions. *How could a baby be so physically beautiful but be so ill internally? How would we care for a child with special needs? How will our church respond to her? How will we provide all of her long-term medical needs? How will our combined income cover all of our expenses?* We were in a financial crisis and did not see any way out. The only thing we could do was pray, trust, and believe that God was going to bring us out. Sadly, the older Kennedi got, the more her health declined over the next twenty-three months. We were willing to do whatever it took to help Kennedi live a quality life.

We put her in a school for children with special needs, called Our Children's House in Irving, Texas. It was an affiliate of Baylor Healthcare System. It was the only daycare that she could receive care from highly capable teachers with medical training. This is where Kennedi received weekly occupational therapy, physical therapy, and speech therapy. Ken took her to school and picked her up every day. He said he would talk to her during the entire ride, and she would stare at him as if she could understand what he was saying. He would always brag about it being his daddy–daughter time. This also meant more medical bills. We distinctly remember opening one medical bill for a half a million dollars. It was a challenging time for our family. We were struggling financially, emotionally, physically, and spiritually. Our faith was being tested, but God continued to make provisions. After juggling to care for both Khaylen and Kennedi for over a year, we learned that we were expecting our third child. This came as a complete surprise because we had been told that we could not have another baby due to medical concerns. We were terrified! My pregnancy was high risk until our son, Kingston was born on February 22, 2005. He was delivered prematurely at eight months due to my health issues. This brought us even more medical bills. The financial burden was becoming overwhelming. I do not remember sleeping much. But we kept our minds on Jesus and His promise that He would never leave us nor forsake us according to Deuteronomy 31:6. Just when we had accepted our new way of living, our new normalcy, we experienced another unexpected blow.

Kennedi's teacher had called us on May 3, 2005, while we were at work and said that she was running a high fever. The center's policy was that children had to be picked up immediately and kept out for at least forty-eight hours or until her doctor determined that she was not contagious. We both took off work to care for Kennedi at home until she could be released to go back to daycare. We took her to her pediatrician the next day, and the doctor indicated that she simply had a common cold and that we needed to give her children Tylenol. She was released to go back to school in a couple of days.

On the morning of May 5, 2005, around 5:00 a.m., I awoke to Ken's gut-wrenching cry, "Kennedi, wake up! Kennedi, wake up!" I was in our bed trying to process what I was hearing. From the sound of Ken's cry, I knew in my heart that she was gone. I went into shock. I felt like my body was paralyzed. I could not move any parts of my body. I could barely scream out, but I got enough breath to scream out, "Is she dead?" It was as if a strong force had me pinned down on our bed. I fought to roll out of my bed to the floor until I had enough strength to run into Kennedi's room, where Ken stood over her body tugging her and asking her to wake up. As soon as I looked at her, I knew she was gone. She had dried up blood on the side of her mouth and some on her pink shirt. I picked up her cold, clammy body and held her tight in my arms and wept until the paramedics and police arrived. When they arrived, one of the paramedics took her out of my arms and laid her in the middle of our living-room floor. He placed his stethoscope on her heart, then looked up at me without saying a word and shook his head no.

Pandemonium broke out as I began to scream and hit the paramedic. I yelled at him, "Please try to save my baby!" I guess a part of me was in denial. Watching him attempt to resuscitate her would have given me a little hope of life. Without saying a word, he simply held me in his arms as I wept. Ken and Khaylen were both being consoled by the other paramedics as they cried. He asked me where I wanted them to put her body until the funeral home arrived. I pointed at the cherry wood bassinet that we kept in the living room. He placed her in it and covered it with one of her baby blankets. I noticed some of the police and paramedics were crying as well. It was something about the death of our little girl that brought grief to everyone. There was not a dry eye in the house.

One of the police officers noticed our newborn baby, Kingston asleep on the couch. With a look of suspicion on his face, he asked Ken and I, "Is the baby on the couch dead too?" With a look of dismay, we both yelled, "No, he's not dead!" With all of the latest news about mother's killing their children, I'm sure they were skeptical when they arrived to residence confronted by a hysterical mother holding her deceased two-year old daughter. It was like a scene from CSI, another officer began to take photos. Another asked if she could walk around our home. Ken immediately ran into the kitchen to call one of his good friends, the late Dr. Jerome McNeil, who began to pray with him over the phone. Afterward he continued to call our other friends and family to notify them of Kennedi's death. I could hear the echo of his voice crying and retelling the story as people kept asking him what happened. Both of our cell phones kept ringing as the news quickly spread.

I noticed that more police officers began to arrive. I finally made the connection that they were handling our home like a crime scene when one of the police officers asked me if I would follow him to his squad car so he could ask me questions about Kennedi. As we walked out of my front door, I could not help but notice all of the yellow crime scene tape wrapped around our house and the other officers redirecting traffic on our street. The officer escorted me to the back of his car and shut the door. He sat in the front seat and turned a bright light to my face and advised me that I was being recorded. I asked, "Sir, am I under arrest?" His response was, "No, this is standard procedures when we are called about a deceased person."

The interrogation began. His first questions was, "Can you explain to me how Kennedi died?" It was followed by several other questions. Even though I was extremely uncomfortable and nervous, I kept my composure and calmly answered all of his questions. I explained her illness and provided him with her neurologist's and pediatrician's contact information. After he finished his interrogation, I was released to go back in the house. As I was lead back in, Ken was being escorted by another officer to be interrogated in the same squad car. Each interrogation session lasted about thirty minutes. After the detectives did phone interviews with Kennedi's pediatrician and neurologist, they confirmed that Kennedi had died of natural causes due to complication from her brain injury. They wrote up their police report accordingly and cleared the scene shortly thereafter.

One of the police officers waited patiently with us as we waited in disbelief for the funeral home mortician to pick up Kennedi's lifeless body. My mother was one of our first family members to arrive. She said she had been waiting to get through all of the police officers that had surrounded our home. Then other family and friends arrived shortly thereafter. With the exception of sniffles, everyone was quiet. Finally, the mortician from the funeral home arrived to pick up our baby. He transferred her body to his stretcher and quietly covered her in a white sheet as he rolled her toward our front door. I stopped him when I laid over Kennedi's stiff body and screamed out the most gut wrenching cry, "My baby, my baby, my baby!" The reality of truth had sunk in. Ken cried as he laid his head on the both of us, then gently pulled me off the bed so that the mortician could push her out of the door. I vividly remember the mortician wiping away tears as he loaded her body in the funeral car. Just like she abruptly came in this world, she abruptly left us in the middle of the night. We felt like a part of us died with her on that day. The pain and shock left us unable to process any rational thoughts. The only way we can describe the loss of a child is to have a whole in your soul for the rest of your life that nothing can seem to fill. As the days progress, we have learned how to cope with our pain.

Kennedi's death date was on my thirty-second birthday, May 5, 2005. Our friends and family did not know whether to wish me a Happy Birthday or give me condolences. Around 4:00 p.m. on my birthday, we found ourselves sitting in front of the funeral home director, Sandra Clark of Sandra Clark

Funeral Home forced to plan for an unexpected funeral for our twenty-three-month-old daughter, Kennedi. We felt like we were in a daze and a maze during the entire planning of Kennedi's funeral. We kept thinking, *We are not supposed to be burying our child. Our child should be burying us.* It was surreal. Today, I still have mixed emotions on my birthday and find it difficult to celebrate.

After speaking with my benefits coordinator at my job, we learned that I did not check the appropriate box to cover our children on my employee life-insurance policy. We did not have life insurance to cover the expenses for Kennedi's funeral and burial. We were already living from paycheck to paycheck, so we didn't have anything in our savings. We were in a financial dilemma; we were heading in a downward financial spiral. There was no one in our family that we could think of who was able to let us borrow at least $10,000 for a funeral. As a matter of fact, it was the first time that we had to carefully consider a list of family and friends who could comfortably loan us that type of money. The more we thought about who we could call to borrow that kind of money from, the shorter our list got. When we finally built up enough nerves to ask the people who *acted* like they had money, they either did not answer our phone calls or did not respond to our cry for help. This made us feel even worse.

We had already read several articles about how over 62% of Americans have less than $1,000 in their savings account, but that day we realized that we were a part of the 62%. While our first thought was how no one we knew had enough money to lend us for a funeral, our second thought was more personal: *We are just as broke as everyone else!* In that moment, we realized that we did not want to spend the rest of our lives in that type of financial position. We knew we needed help, but we felt so helpless. We found ourselves doing a lot of praying and crying until Jesus answered. The benefit coordinator from my job called me a couple of days after Kennedi's death and said the company was going to pay for Kennedi's entire funeral and burial. The funds came out of an employee crisis fund account. They told us to make an itemized list of all the expenses associated with the funeral and her burial. At the time, we were still suffering psychologically from the trauma of her death, but we continued to thank God for His faithfulness.

After Kennedi's funeral on May 10, 2005, our marriage was never the same. In order to cope with our loss, Ken began to work even harder and longer hours at the church, and I began to completely shut down emotionally. The guilt for failing to protect and save our only daughter kept me in a dark place. I kept seeing visions of her with that dried-up blood on the side of her mouth that had dripped down her pink shirt. She would suddenly appear on a regular basis. It seemed liked she was trying to talk to me, but no words would come out of her mouth. In my desperation for answers, I would ask her, "Kennedi, what are you trying to tell me?" My therapist explained to me that I was experiencing trauma, which is a normal reaction to the terrifying event. Along with Kennedi's sudden appearances, I kept reliving the terror of finding her lifeless body.

I had nightmares every night, severe anxiety, and constant questions of what could've caused her death. *Did she have a massive seizure? Did she choke on her own saliva or vomit? Did she have an infection?* I felt like I was losing my mind. Ken couldn't seem to reach me. I was scared. After being diagnosed with posttraumatic stress syndrome, I knew it was best to take a leave of absence from my job. I visited a therapist on a weekly basis to help cope with my pain. This was a major turning point in our lives. I began to write a daily journal about everything that I was feeling. The more I wrote, the more I began to see life clearer as I started to come out of the fog of loss, grief, shock, trauma, and depression. Ken and I began to have weekly family meetings about how to get out of our financial crisis.

In our weekly discussions, Ken reminded me of all the millions of dollars that I had helped manage for major corporations in my career as an accountant. He told me if I could help corporations maintain their financial records, make important financial decisions, meet the company's financial goals, and prepare budgets, why couldn't we do it for our own finances? We had decided at that moment that we would be in full control of our finances, instead of allowing our finances to control us. It had been controlling us for the last couple of years, and we were ready to give it all to God. Our weekly financial meetings were very similar to business meetings. Ken was the CEO of the "Hollingshed Household" and I was the accountant and business manager of the "Hollingshed Household".

In his book, *Getting Along with Each Other*, author Rev. Richard Strauss uses an acronym for the word "PLAN" to help remember the four principles associated with putting a plan into action. **P** - Pray, **L** - Listen and Learn, **A** - Answer Positively, **N** - Note the Critic's Needs. We thought about this short, but powerful acronym every time we met to discuss our personal finances. We wrote down our vision of our financial goals and a detailed plan of how we were going to execute the principals. Then prayed over the plan and worked it with expectancy. We made sure we listened very carefully to each other's concerns and ideas as we worked together to put our plain into action. We always recapped our plans and made sure all questions had been answered. Before we closed our meetings with prayer, we made sure we took detailed notes of our discussions, any changes and revisions to our plans. Not only did the weekly meetings help us to stay focused, but they helped us to develop great communication skills in our marriage. One of our goals was to stop renting and to purchase our own home. We were very specific with the type of home that we wanted, even down to having a big backyard with a lake view.

We pulled our credit report and listed each debt in the order of the highest interest rate. We called every single creditor on our credit report, explained why we were in debt, and made payment arrangements. After we shared our story, some of them forgave our debt, some allowed us to make minimum payments, and some allowed us to settle with an agreed-upon amount. Once we paid off our first bill, we took our money that we were sending to that creditor and sent it to the next one on the list. This method is called debt stacking. Use the debt stacking method chart listed in the appendix as guide to help you with paying off your debts.

We were blessed to close on our house in August 2005, ninety days after Kennedi's death. Our house is a lakeside property that sits on Lake Lewisville, and our backyard is about one acre. We continued to work toward our financial goals and plans. God did much more than what we expected. It took Kennedi's birth to shake us, her illness to propel us, and her death to awaken us. Now we want to share our financial journey with you so that you can attain continued financial growth in a way that most Christians never learn because their churches do not realize the importance of this teaching on finances. Managing our money according to God's biblical principles has brought us so much peace and joy. We have used these same principles from this forty-day financial renewal book to help us exercise discipline in our spending habits and to change our mind-set about how we handle our finances.

By no means is this a "get rich quick," "name it and claim it," or "prosperity gospel" book. But rather, it is a book intended to reflect the success that we attained with our money when we started trusting God with our finances. We have combined the principles of God's truth on biblical stewardship along with accounting and finance knowledge as the catalyst for living in financial renewal. Financial renewal is a continual process. We have continued to use principles from this book throughout our marriage as we go through different seasons of life. Even in the midst of writing this book we experienced unexpected financial hardships that prompted us to revisit principles from this book. We believe you will experience the same as you go through the forty-day financial renewal process.

It is our intent to empower people based on our personal experience, practical insight, and understanding of biblical truth. It is imperative for everyone in the Body of Christ to understand how to manage their finances God's way as well as to press their way toward that higher prize, which is in Jesus Christ our Lord (Philippians 3:14). No one is exempt from life crisis. We are living witnesses that you can survive anything with the power of prayer. You are organisms designed to grow. We are sharing this fruit of the vine with you because it is our passion as servants of the Lord. The Bible declares that "faith comes by hearing, and hearing by the word of God" (Romans 10:17). The devil uses our lack of understanding and misconceptions about money to keep us impoverished spiritually, mentally, and financially. If you really want to know the test of obedience, then take time to not only read this book, but also take time to be a part of those who are not only "hearers, but doers of the word. (James 7:22)

Deepening Your Understanding of and Your relationship with God Through the Power of Prayer

Prayer is personal communication between you and God. It helps you to truly know God and His character. God hears your prayers, and they never go unheard by Him. Supplication is to beseech, petition, or appeal for Him to do or provide something for yourself or others. It brings God joy when His children ask Him for help. 1 John 5:14 says, "This is the confidence we have in approaching God: that if we ask anything according to his will, he hears us." God hears your prayers and knows exactly what you need. So, when your prayers go unanswered, that does not mean that He does not want to bless you. It means that it may not be in line with His will for your life. Prayer is the starting point for good stewardship because it requires spending time listening and talking with God.

Biblical Stewardship is a lifestyle that involves a deeper understanding of your relationship with God, yourself, and others. The call to stewardship is a way of life that leads us to become disciples of Christ. In a more formal definition of stewardship, it is the careful and responsible management of something entrusted to one's care. God expects you to be a responsible manager of His resources that He has entrusted to you. Spiritual growth and renewal are essential and life-long processes of the life of any dedicated Christian. Stewardship leads you to recognize the blessings you have received from God and to show your gratitude for the gifts that you have received by returning to Him a portion of your time, talent, and treasure.

Our desire is for you to be wealthy. There is a difference between being wealthy and rich. Wealthy people have an abundance of assets that far exceed their liabilities. They make wise choices and decisions with their money that allows them to accumulate even more over time. Rich people typically acquire their money instantly—by inheritance, lottery, professional sports, or entertainment contracts. Sadly, the money can go just as fast if they lack money-management skills & knowledge. Statistically, almost half of lottery winners spend most or all their winnings within five years. On the other hand, wealthy people know how to manage their money and constantly work at building wealth that will last throughout several generations.

This book will help you to understand the reason why you need strategies for setting the financial goals you want to achieve and the steps you can take to achieve them. You will learn how to make the best use of your resources to raise your standard of living and create financial victory that can be passed on to future generations. We would like to ask you, your church, your family, your friends and/or small groups to take this forty-day journey and find the hidden treasures by putting God first in your finances. We have learned over the years from our personal experiences that new converts, church leaders, and members of the Body of Christ must be trained and equipped to be faithful stewards to maximize their full positive potential in the stewardship of their personal finances and the kingdom. We pray that this book will provide hope, inspiration, and encouragement to everyone in the Body of Christ who needs a financial renewal.

During the next forty days, you will be in a financial renewal process. You will hear about more opportunities to do God's work in your personal finances. You will be asked to reflect on your covenant with God as it relates to your money. The covenant is God's kingdom-building program. You will be challenged to trust God with what He has made available to you. You will make impactful financial decisions related to your giving, spending, and plan for your financial future.

Just like Jesus, many others in the Bible, and we were tempted; you too will be tempted to hold back your tithes and offerings during these next forty days of financial renewal process. Jesus overcame temptation through grace and strength from God. Jesus trusted that God would give Him the strength to overcome trials and tribulations. When He was tempted by the devil, Jesus depended on the power of God to see Him through. His victory over sin and death has given us the opportunity to hear God's word and believe so that we may have everlasting life (John 5:24). We encourage you to use this book as your guide and personal covenant with God as you go through the next forty days of financial renewal.

RENEWING MY UNDERSTANDING OF MONEY

*Why should fools have money in hand to buy wisdom,
when they are not able to understand it.*
~Proverbs 17:16

In our financial crisis, we came to realize that "life can turn on a dime". That saying came alive in our situation. We were seemingly living a life free of any major debts or issues. In fact, we were spending our money freely because that was the only way we knew. We didn't have an in-depth understanding of money because of the way we were raised. As a Baby Boomer, Ken grew up in a culture that taught him to work hard and earn as much as possible in his younger years to create wealth for his retirement years. And as a Generation X, I grew up in a culture that taught me to spend, spend, and spend. Sadly, I didn't learn the consequences until it was too late.

Like us, many Christians have a misunderstanding about money. Many recognize that God has blessed them with money, but oftentimes they forget why He blesses them with money. Usually a major life crisis that affects your finances forces you to think about money in a new way. When you have a proper understanding of money, you can take action instead of reacting to a financial crisis or hardship. But, to get ahead financially, you need not only a good understanding of biblical principles, you also need to understand money, economics, the economic system, and how it affects you as a consumer and a citizen.

Economics is the study of how our society uses limited resources such as workers, machines, factories, raw materials, etc. to satisfy our unlimited needs and wants. The economic system is the structure in which the resources are turned into goods and services to address our unlimited needs and wants. There has been an economic system since the biblical days. Throughout the Bible, God teaches us about the economic system in which people sold cattle, sheep, doves, and other resources in exchange for money to address the people's unlimited needs and wants. (John 2:14) Even God's principle of giving is a part of the economic system. (Proverbs 3:9) Things have not changed much since the biblical days. Today, people continue to have unlimited needs and wants. Oftentimes we confuse our unlimited needs with our unlimited wants. Your needs are the things that are ordinarily required for the survival of human life such as food, water, air, housing, medication, etc. Your wants are the items you would like to have, but are not essential for keeping you alive.

God's desire is to give you the things that you need, not necessarily the things that you want. According to Philippians 4:19, "God will meet all of our needs according to the riches of His glory in Christ Jesus". Economists spend a lot of time researching, collecting, analyzing data, and monitoring economic trends to examine how our society distributes resources that produce the goods and services that meet our needs as consumers. Their studies also prove that we are living in times of economic uncertainty and wealth inequality in America. In biblical times people faced similar disparities. Isaiah 1:17 says, "Learn to do good; seek justice, correct oppression; bring justice to the fatherless, plead the widow's cause." We live in a culture that tells us that a normal life is to be rich, and that the people with the most money have the most power. This is the reason why there are so many people living fear-driven lives. Many Americans are afraid of losing their material possessions and their standard of living, and rightfully so. Far too many people are seeking identity in their money. The problem with this thought process is when they lose their money or experience a reduction in income, they tend to lose their identity along with it.

When you think about money, what are the first thoughts that come to your mind? Most people have different perspectives of money. If you put several people in a room together and ask them their thoughts about money, each person is going to express different types of emotions based on their understanding of money and their current financial situation. Your feelings about money dictate how you manage your money. Let's face it, most people immediately associate money with their financial obligations. It is viewed simply as a means of survival. When it comes to money, most people think about when they are going to get more, how they are going to get it, and what they are going to do with it once they get it. If this is the extent of your thoughts about money, you will find it difficult to put yourself in a better financial position.

To understand money is to know that the monetary system is where goods and services are indirectly exchanged using money. There are three functions of money: 1. A medium of exchange, 2. Unit of account, and 3. Store of value. I'm sure you are probably thinking: *What are they talking about? Do I really need to know all of this to manage my finances?* The answer is emphatically Yes! A medium of exchange means that buyers give items to sellers when they want to purchase goods and services. For instance, when you buy a new pair of shoes from a shoe store, the store gives you the shoes in exchange for your money. A unit of account is a guide that people use to post prices and record debts. This means that you are using money as the unit of account to measure the value of the shoes. A store of value is an item that people can use to transfer purchasing power from the present to the future. This means if you decided to save your money for six months before you purchase the shoes, your money will still hold its value over time. In other words, you can save your money for later use and it will not lose value.

As a high school business education teacher, I feel that it is important for my students to understand early on that the monetary system is the foundation for running a business. When teaching personal finance, I typically cover the meaning and function of money before I get into budgeting, saving, investing, etc. I believe understanding money is key to planning for the future. One year I had an opportunity to take my high school business classes to the Federal Reserve Bank in Dallas for a guided tour. They were able to see interactive exhibits, study historical currency and learn more about the Federal Reserve. Their perspectives about money changed after that experience. They began to see money as more than a means of survival, but as more of an asset.

We wish more adults would take time to learn how money works. We believe it would eliminate some of the discomfort when the subject of money comes up in the church. The word "money" seems to be a taboo in the church. One of the most misquoted bible verses is "Money is the root of all evil". Money was never intended to be evil, yet, every time money is mentioned in the church, we literally see people frowning, angry, fearful, or disapproval. 1 Timothy 6:10 says, "For the *love* of money is a root of all kinds of evil. Some people, eager for money, have wandered from the faith and pierced themselves with many griefs." Keep in mind that God blesses you with money as a resource to bless Him, yourself, and others.

When you do not understand money, it can be intimidating to talk about. One of the reasons for my passion for teaching financial literacy comes from my observation of people's reactions, thoughts, and relationship with money. Renewing your understanding of money is a powerful tool that will help you grow spiritually, know where you stand financially, build your financial future, and be an effective financial manager.

SMARTER GOAL WORKSHEET

Today's Date:_____/_____/_____
Start Date:_____/_____/_____
End Date:_____/_____/_____
Financial Goal:_____

Setting financial goals is an essential part of life. In order to create your own success, you must be specific about what you want to accomplish. It's time to start "working smarter not harder". Verify that your financial goal is smarter by answering the following questions.

Specific: What type of financial breakthrough do you need from God?

Measurable: How will you know when you are getting closer to the financial breakthrough?

Attainable: Is achieving financial renewal realistic with effort and commitment? Do you have the resources and support to remain committed? If not, how will you get them?

Relevant: Why is this financial renewal significant to your life? Why should this happen right now?

Timely: What will you do to keep yourself focused and motivated during the next forty days?

Evaluable: How will you know when you are financially renewed?

Rewarding: How will you reward yourself for your commitment to the covenant?

PART I
Renewing My Covenant with God

And I will establish my covenant between me and you and your seed after you in their generations for an everlasting covenant.
—Genesis 17:7–8

DAY 1
A New Covenant with God

Today is day one of your financial renewal. It is so important that you start this financial renewal process with a renewed covenant with God. You may be wondering why you need to renew your covenant. First, let us explain what a covenant is. A covenant is a contract or agreement between two or more parties. Any time there is a contract in place, you must know the terms and conditions so that you know and understand your responsibilities. When we think of a covenant with God, we think of a marriage. It is a lifetime union between two people. It takes two people to get married, but legally it only takes one person to get out of a marriage. Unfortunately, we live in a society where couples are quick to divorce and quick to breach the covenant. Similarly, many Christians are quick to break their covenant with God. Although they know the right things to do, they fail to be obedient. God views breaking the covenant with Him as a sin. James 4:17 says, "If anyone, then, knows the good they ought to do and doesn't do it, it is sin for them."

Your covenant with God is sacred. God communicates to you through your covenant with Him. His covenant redeems you, rewards you, and promises you eternal life. Many Christians struggle with unbelief and doubt in their spirits, particularly when it comes to finances. This is the main reason why many disobey God in the area of paying tithes and offerings. It does not necessarily mean that believers do not love God; it simply means that many believers do not always trust Him with their finances. It is easy to come up with a lot of excuses why God cannot be trusted. Truth is the basis of trust. Trust helps to develop a stronger relationship with Him. *When you do not trust God with your finances, it creates a spiritual gap between you and Him.* Any time there is a gap, it leaves a foothold for the enemy. We are all guilty of it. You may have broken or breached your covenant with God, but we thank God that we serve a God who shows us so much grace, mercy, and forgiveness.

When Israel arrived at the base of Mount Sinai, they discovered that God had chosen this place to enter into a covenant with them. Moses went up the mountain to meet with God, and God immediately explained His intention for Israel. "Now if you obey me fully and keep my covenant, then out of all nations you will be my treasured possession. Although the whole earth is mine, you will be for me a kingdom of priests and a holy nation. These are the words you are to speak to the Israelites" (Exodus 19:5–6). God had a master plan for the Israelites that could only be fulfilled through His covenant. He has a master plan for your life as well.

That master plan includes the finances that you are blessed with. We had to learn that even during millions of dollars of debt, we had to keep our covenant with God. We must admit there were times when we were tempted to do it our way, which could have compromised our covenant with God, but we remained faithful. At times, it seemed like we were sinking deeper and deeper beyond the point of no return. Every day was financially overwhelming. There was no eating out, movies, or vacations. Our leisure time seemed to be gone forever. Some days our prayer for financial deliverance seemed to go unheard, but we knew we had to live out the covenant in order to receive His promises. God wanted us to achieve financial freedom.

All of our lives are filled with contractual relationships that have rights and obligations. Virtually every phase of our life is governed in a way or another by contracts. This is true of our private lives and our business lives as well. (Hiscox, Spandel and Lewis 2004) When you buy or lease your home, borrow money from a bank, or purchase certain goods and services, you are required to sign a contract. These contracts are designed to provide you with the assurance that each party agrees to perform some type of act. If either of the parties involved in the contractual agreement does not fulfill the contractual promises, they are subject to pay for any damages caused by the breach of contact. As a result, you risk losing your home, car, job, or whatever you used as collateral. There are similar conditions and consequences for keeping and breaking your covenant with God.

When you are not in covenant with God, He will allow you to suffer the consequences of your sin. When you are in covenant with Him, He will bless you. God wants you to be in covenant with Him during this financial renewal process. Like everything else in your daily walk with God, you must be in a covenant with God. Allow God to do something supernatural with your finances. Renew your covenant with God by completing the financial covenant agreement.

Prayer:

Today, Lord, help me to understand the covenantal principles and my covenant with You. You rule over every part of creation, and therefore I must submit to Your kingdom agenda. I realize that Your provisions and promises flow through Your covenant. Bless and anoint my financial covenant agreement. Amen.

Reading:

"The Lord covenants to make Israel a peculiar treasure, a kingdom of priests, and a holy nation—The people sanctify themselves—The Lord appears on Sinai amid fire, smoke, and earthquakes" (Exodus 19:5–6).

Application:

What are your inner thoughts about the covenant that you have made with God as the ruler over your finances?

FINANCIAL COVENANT AGREEMENT

I, _____, commit myself today to start and finish the forty-day financial renewal. I vow to put forth my best effort to *finish* and to stay focused. If I remain positive and abide in You, I know I will receive financial victory. During this financial renewal process,

I want to accomplish the following: (Be specific)

I will measure my progress by doing the following:

I will reward myself for remaining committed for 40 days with the following:

I will be accountable to the following partner(s)?

_____
Your Signature

_____
Date

DAY 2
Under New Management

You have taken a big step toward your financial future. Hopefully, you have completed your financial covenant agreement and have decided to put your finances under the new management of God as you go through this financial renewal experience. You are highly skilled at doing it your way; now let us teach you how to do it God's way. We realize that it takes courage to turn over your money to a new manager. After all, you earned it, and so you feel like it belongs to you. We certainly know how you feel. It is that feeling you get when you pull up to one of your favorite places to dine or shop only to find a sign posted in the window that reads "Under New Management." Whenever a business is under new management, it means there has been a change of ownership or a total change of tenant if it's a rented business. A change in ownership typically means there are going to be some major changes to follow.

If it were your favorite restaurant, chances are there will be different servers, different menus, different decor, and a different atmosphere. All of the changes threaten your sense of familiarity and comfort with the restaurant. You have probably experienced the same feeling on a new job when you got a new manager or principal, or in church when you got a new pastor. Most people are initially uncomfortable experiencing change. Real change can make you feel like you want to run away from or avoid feelings of discomfort. Your feelings of discomfort are normal because the brain is wired to reinforce what you believe to be true. That's why real change starts with you renewing your mind. Putting your finances under the new management of God means that you will need to change your thoughts and approach to how you manage your finances. Jesus has a stewardship approach to money. The stewardship approach is that God owns everything; as believers, we are simply managers of His resources. If this is your first time changing how you manage your finances, it is going be uncomfortable until you get used to your new lifestyle.

Stewardship expresses your willingness to be obedient to God and your commitment to manage your finances according to biblical principles. Essentially, you are giving God what already belongs to Him. When you embrace the biblical view of stewardship, you are giving God glory, honor, and praise with your finances. The Bible makes it clear that all things were created by Him and for Him (Colossians 1:16) One of the most important principles about your finances is to understand that it all belongs to God. As a manager of God's resources, you are responsible for overseeing the resources that God has provided you. Being an effective manager of God's resources reminds me of my roles as business manager when I served at two major radio stations in Dallas. One of my many responsibilities was to ensure that the company's financial goals were being met in order to profitably provide services to its customers. I didn't own the companies, but the owner expected and relied upon me to manage it appropriately and responsibly. In the business world, there are key managerial skills to be a good manager. Effective managers need skills that fall into three basic categories: *interpersonal, technical, and conceptual*. (Bovee and Thill 2001) Likewise, effective stewardship requires your *time, talent and resources*.

Many Christians struggle with the fact that God owns everything. In Luke 16:11, the parable is focused on a steward who is accused of wasting the master's resources, and the mismanagement causes the following response: "So if you have not been trustworthy in handling worldly wealth, who will trust you with true riches?" Jesus encourages His followers to be generous with their wealth so that they can receive all of His heavenly rewards that come with being good stewards of His earthly resources. There are two points of the steward's action in this text: (1) He provided a negative example of misusing his master's resources and losing his job. (2) Jesus condemned the behavior of the steward for being selfish. (vv. 3–7)

The steward tried to advance himself through the favor of his master's debtors by reducing their debts and hoping for positive treatment from them after his dismissal. This is a reminder that you should make wise use of the resources and opportunities that God gives you. During this forty-day financial renewal experience, you will need to commit to putting your finances under the new management of God. Living under the management of God often requires radical choices.

Being under new management seeks to transition you from the destructive patterns of old desires to the new and different ways of managing your finances, which will ultimately give you the financial peace that you deserve. This type of living is to reflect the qualities and character of God. It will transition you to being a person who walks by faith and not by sight (2 Corinthians 5:7). While financial renewal is a tremendous blessing, what matters more are the blessings that are unseen. Your focus should not be on the tangible things that you can see such as our finances and other material possessions, rather you should focus on the things not seen. Tangible things that you can see are temporary. According to 2 Corinthians 4:18, "So we fix our eyes not on what is seen, but on what is unseen, since what is seen is temporary, but what is unseen is eternal." You will be able manage your finances and see it not as an end in itself, but as a means to advance the kingdom of Christ.

Prayer:

Today, Lord, my finances are under Your management. I release my finances to You according to your principles and truths. As I start my financial renewal experience, speak to me and teach me how to be a good manager of what you have entrusted me with. Amen.

Reading:

Luke 16:11: "So if you have not been trustworthy in handling worldly wealth, who will trust you with true riches?"

Application:

List all of your income and expenses on the budget template located at the back of this book. Subtract your total expenses from your total income to get your net income. Can God trust you to manage His finances from this day forward?

DAY 3
First Fruits

Tithing has been a major principle since the biblical days. There were only two types of income that were tithable: One was from agricultural production. The second type of tithable income was the increase of animals. (Associates for Scriptural Knowledge 2014) A tenth of all agricultural produce such as fruits or vegetables was used as a tithe. The main source of currency was sheep, cattle, or goats. Cattle were often used for trade. Most of the transactions were made on the barter system. (Leviticus 27:30) In the twenty-first century, many Christians struggle with tithing and feel that it is overrated. Therefore, some Christians refuse to be obedient to the Lord. Tithing was intended to be a joy and a blessing, not a burden. Being a faithful tither is a spiritual practice that requires discipline and obedience.

To be a good manager, you must develop strong management skills. Management skills put you in full control of the resources that God has entrusted you with. He trusts you to make the right decisions and to carry them out. You will benefit from your good decisions. Just like in the business world, money management is a three-step process that requires (1) planning, (2) acting, and (3) evaluating. The same principles apply to managing our finances. The planning stage includes you identifying your financial goals including making your tithes a priority in your finances. *The action stage is putting your plan into action.* You must work your plan with expectancy that you will face obstacles that may keep you from sticking to your plan. If you get off your plan, get back on it. There is no need to beat yourself up about it. The evaluation stage allows you to assess your progress as you go through the process of managing financial resources. This is your opportunity to determine what worked, what didn't work, and how you can do better next time. For an example, if you typically pay your tithes weekly but find it to be a challenge to pay it weekly, try paying it biweekly or through an auto bank draft once a month. Evaluate your financial performance regularly so that you learn how to make improvements.

"First fruits" refers to the first portion of the harvest which is given to God. Giving the first fruits was also a way of expressing trust in God's provision. According to Proverbs 3:9–10, believers are to use our financial resources to honor God. We do this by trusting God and giving Him the first of our resources. This is how we show our gratitude for all that He has given us. Honoring the Lord goes much further than just attending church and stating that we are believers. Tithing has been known since the Old Testament times. For example, it is recorded in Genesis 14:17–20 that Abraham paid tithes to Melchizedek. Through the prophet Malachi, the Lord declared, "Bring ye all the tithes into the storehouse, that there may be meat in mine house, and prove me now herewith, saith the Lord of hosts, if I will not open you the windows of heaven, and pour you out a blessing, that there shall not be room enough to receive it" (Malachi 3:10).

Ken and I typically meet every week to calculate our household expenses. We start out by calculating 10 percent of our gross monthly income off the top and pay our tithes first before we pay other bills. We pay ourselves 5–10 percent by putting aside in our savings account. Then we pay our bills with the 80 percent remaining in our budget. It took some time for us to make the transitions in our budget, but after a while, it became second nature. Sometimes unexpected expenses come up that causes us to have to make temporary changes to our budget. Use the budget template in the appendix section to calculate and manage your 10-10-80 plan. Take the time to list the amount of your first fruit (tithe) that you owe God each month as well as your other monthly obligations.

If you are a believer in the Word of God, you should be a faithful tither. You should be giving 10 percent of your income to your local church as your tithes. How much are you currently giving to your local church? Review the tithe chart located in the appendix to determine where you fall on the percentage column. Are you paying at least 10 percent or more? If not, make a commitment to gradually increase your giving to three or more percentages. If you are already giving 10 percent, make a commitment to increase your percentages to three or more percentages and/or increase your offerings.

If you do not have an emergency fund account, we suggest you make a commitment to putting aside at least $25 a month toward building a $500 emergency fund for those unexpected expenses that may pop up. This is separate from your 10 percent that goes toward your savings account. As you plan to give God your first fruit, work your plan with expectancy that you will face unexpected expenses. Most financial experts suggest that you build up your emergency fund to cover at least 3 to 6 months of living expenses. Having an emergency fund in place prevents you from having to spend from your budgeted expenses.

Prayer:

Today, Lord, I realize that according to your Word I should honor You with my first fruits. Forgive me if I have mismanaged Your resources in the past. Help me to remain committed to my financial plan. Thank you for the opportunity to management what belongs to You. Amen.

Reading:

Proverbs 3:9–10: "Honor the Lord with your wealth, with the first fruits of all your crops; then your barns will be filled to overflowing, and your vats will brim over with new wine."

Application:

Calculate 10% of your gross monthly income. (For example: If your monthly gross income is $2,000.00 a month, you owe God $200.00 a month in tithe ($2,000 x 0.10 = $200.00). List the amount of your "first fruit" (tithe) that you owe God each month. If you have not been paying this amount, what adjustments will you make to your budget?

DAY 4
Write the Vision

God gives us a vision as a supernatural appearance to convey His revelation. Ken is a visionary leader. Visionary leaders tend to be focused, optimistic, enthusiastic, and they inspire those around them. His strong sense of vision is what has shaped not only our household, but also our church. It has brought order and peace to our lives. In order to accomplish our financial goals, we had to write our well-organized and detailed personal financial plan. We started our financial plan with a family vision statement. Ken suggested coming up with our family vision statement shortly after Kennedi passed. Our family vision statement is, "Use your God-given gifts to equip, inspire, love and to leave a legacy." Our family restates our vision statement during our prayer time and monthly budgeting meetings. We wrote down our vision of our financial goals and a detailed plan on how we planned on meeting our specific goals. We ordered a copy of our credit reports and reviewed our credit history so we could see our financial position.

We calculated our net worth by developing a list of all of our current assets and liabilities. *Assets* are things you own and *liabilities* are the things you owe. We subtracted all of our liabilities from our total assets, which gave us a clear picture of our net worth. We created a filing system for all of our financial records and put them in due-date order. We listed all of our current monthly income and expenses so that we could develop a realistic budget. We created a monthly budget and reviewed it regularly. This is how we strategically began to work our way out of our financial wilderness. A financial plan allows you to control your financial situation. It is your spending plan for the use of the money that God has blessed you to manage over time based on your financial goals and your expected income. When Ken and I decided that we were going to get out of our financial hardship after the illness and subsequent death of Kennedi, we began to write down our vision of our financial goals and a detailed plan.

Make your financial vision plain, and watch God bless your plan! In Habakkuk 2:2, Habakkuk had been waiting patiently for an answer from God. He finally gets his answer that the time for the destruction of the Jewish polity by the Chaldeans was drawing near. Therefore, God commanded him to write down the vision in the most legible characters and in the plainest language so that everyone who reads can flee from the upcoming threat. Write down your financial plan and goals. When you write it down, your mind will embrace what it sees. If you only think about it, it will only remain a mere thought.

What is your net worth? Determine your net worth by taking inventory of what you own and what you owe. Use the net worth statement in the appendix to take a financial inventory of all of your assets, such as your home, car, investment accounts, bank accounts, equipment, jewelry, etc. and your liabilities, such as mortgage loans, car loans, school loans, credit cards, cell phone contract, etc. When you add up the value of all of your assets and subtract your liabilities, this is your *net worth*. Write down your short-term and long-range financial goals and make it plain. Financial renewal requires spiritual guidance, vision, planning, and organization.

In his book, *Supervision Today!*, author, Stephen P Robbins says, "Your vision is a realistic, credible, and attainable view of the future that grows out of and improves on the present." Take time today to complete your monthly budget plan located in the appendix. Your budget plan will guide you through all your financial decisions. Your personal saving plan should be a part of your budget as it is a very crucial aspect of financial planning. It consists of income that you put aside for future use. This is your strategic plan for using your money to reach your bigger, long-term goals. Keep in mind that your financial goals will change as you continue to grow financially. Economic conditions, such as job choices and your financial status will affect your earning potential. Changes in technology will also affect the way you live and spend your money, which is why it is so important for you to keep up with emerging technology. Your thoughts must move to an action so that it becomes your reality. You will see your financial plan begin to line up with your vision.

Prayer:

Today, Lord, I will be a good manager of Your resources. Knowing that my life and service as a steward is being evaluated by You, I will create a budget plan that lists all of my income and expenses. This plan is unique to my financial situation. Bless it, Lord. Amen.

Reading:

Habakkuk 2:2. Then the Lord replied: "Write down the revelation and make it plain on tablets so that a herald may run with it."

Application:

What is your family vision statement? If you do not have a vision statement, create one today.

DAY 5
Financial Equality

Financial inequality is no secret and has been an ongoing problem in the United States for a very long time. In case you are not familiar with financial inequality, allow us to explain it to you. Financial or economic inequality is the differences found in various measures of the economic well-being among individuals in a specific group in a population of people. Typically, economists measure the economic disproportion in three ways: wealth, income, and consumption. Wealth is the abundance of our valuable material possessions. Income is the consumption and savings opportunity that is expressed with our monetary provisions. Consumption is our individual purchase of goods and services. In the United States, there is a major gap between the rich and the poor, and it is growing rapidly. That is where the saying "the rich get richer and poor get poorer" comes from.

Per the Pew Research Center,

> The black-white income gap in the U.S. has persisted. The difference in median household incomes between whites and blacks has grown from about $19,000 in 1967 to roughly $27,000 in 2011 (as measured in 2012 dollars). Median

black household income was 59% of median white household income in 2011, up modestly from 55% in 1967; as recently as 2007, black income was 63% of white income.1

This research proves that there is a distinct financial divide between races, which is a serious problem in the United States that needs to be addressed. Ken and I cannot solve the problems of financial inequality, but we can offer some solutions to the problem. We truly believe financial literacy is a part of the solution. Financial literacy is the understanding of the basic knowledge and skills needed to manage financial resources. Being financially literate means you are knowledgeable of the financial management skills needed to prepare you for your financial future while avoiding the pitfalls of debt. Knowledge is power!

As I speak on the importance of being financially literate at different church conferences, I meet a lot of adults who say they wished they had learned about financial literacy in high school. In candid conversations and discussions, only about 5–10 percent say they were taught about money in high school, the others said they had to learn by trial and error. About 40 percent of them admitted to keeping a budget and tracking their spending. However, over 50 percent admitted to living paycheck to paycheck, which makes it difficult for them to have a savings. Many people do not have a working knowledge of how to accumulate wealth to establish a financial legacy. Those who lack the knowledge and understanding of money and financial principles experience higher interest in auto/consumer loans, higher debt delinquencies, lower savings, and lower homeownership rate. When we purchased our first home in 2005, it was a blessing to have a good understanding of financial principles. Our knowledge and understanding[1] empowered us to negotiate great interest rates and monthly payments.

Financial inequality has been an issue since the biblical days. The Bible discusses the structures that oppressed the poor. It is especially common in the Old Testament. It talks a lot about giving to the poor and treating them fair in court (Proverbs 22:22–23), so that they will not be discriminated against. Let's face it, most Christians realize that there is a major wealth gap not only by race, but in the Body of Christ as well. Many of our congregations are distinctly divided between the haves and the have-nots. Because the gap between the rich and the poor in the United States is growing considerably, there is a larger number of people in need.

It is imperative for Christians to treat those in need with the heart of God. People need to hear the Gospel and how Christ died for us so we can have eternal life. According to John 3:16, "For God so loved the world that he gave his one and only Son, that whoever believes in him shall not perish but have eternal life." One way our ministry shares with those is need is through our ongoing partnership with the Salvation Army in Dallas. We have held a consistent worship service twice a month for approximately one hour on their premises in the chapel for over six years. We use this time to preach, teach, and provide care packages to those who live in the homeless shelter on-site. We also provide transportation to our worship service as needed.

You must navigate in society with a biblical view of wealth and poverty. It is imperative that every Christian faces the

---

[1] Drew DeSilver, "5 Facts about Economic Inequality," Pew Research Center RSS, 2014, http://www.pewresearch.org/fact-tank/2014/01/07/5-facts- about-economic-inequality/.

issues of financial inequality first by learning and understanding financial literacy. Incorporate financial literacy in your home with your children, in your church, in your local library and community so that everyone in the Body of Christ can accumulate wealth and pass it down to the next generation. Do not get distracted by the wealth gap; rather, refocus your heart and mind on what pleases God.

Prayer:

Today, Lord, I pray for financial equality in America. We know some of your people are suffering financially. Even though income is not being distributed equally among people, we know that You will bless us with a righteously transformed America. Amen.

Reading:

Proverbs 22:7. "The rich rule over the poor, and the borrower is slave to the lender."

Application:

How have you witnessed financial inequality? List your specific concerns of income inequality:

DAY 6
God's Power to Do More

There is nothing worse than feeling like you are being control by your debt. In other words, you are being "controlled by your debt" when you are at a constant state of worry, stress, and anxiety about having a lack of money to cover all of your debt. Do not throw in the towel! There is hope, and there is a way for you to be in complete control of your debt. "Do not be anxious about anything, but in everything, by prayer and petition, with thanksgiving, present your requests to God. And the peace of God, which transcends all understanding, will guard your hearts and your minds in Christ Jesus." (Philippians 4:6–7) In Ephesians 3:20, Paul says, "Now to him who is able to do immeasurably more than all we ask or imagine, according to his power that is at work within us." Paul prays for believers to be strengthened by the Holy Spirit. He talks about the awesomeness of God and how God can do above and beyond all that they could ask for or think of.

Knowing that God is working on our behalf should cause us to bring Him glory. Ken and I have been in so much debt that we literally felt like we would never get out. At one time, we were getting collection calls all day long, and our stacks of collection letters grew every day. During Kennedi's illness, our main focus was paying for her several different medicines, her doctor visits, weekly daycare tuition, and all of the emergency-room visits. We had to let several bills go unpaid so that we could pay for her medical needs. We tried to get assistance, but we were told that we made too much money. We never understood their calculations because every time we calculated all of her expenses, Kennedi's expenses alone far exceeded our combined monthly income. We even tried applying for disability for Kennedi and was denied. At times, we felt helpless and hopeless. Although there were times when we were frustrated about our financial situation, we remained faithful to God and continued to remain prayerful.

One day we got an unexpected call from a debt collector who informed us that one of Kennedi's medical bills in the amount of a half a million dollars had been forgiven. This was one of our major debts, so it took a tremendous load off us when God eliminated that debt. God has the power to do more than we could have ever imagined. This was one of so many blessings that God has bestowed upon our lives. According to a new study by Pew Charitable Trusts, 80 percent of Americans have some form of debt. This means that personal debt is a serious problem in the United States. One of the main causes of high debt is credit card debt.

Many people find it difficult to refuse a new credit card offer. Often times they are easy to get, but hard to pay off due to high interest rates. We have met many people who are in serious credit card debt in the Body of Christ and in desperate need of debt relief. We are living witnesses that God can do things beyond our wildest dreams. Oftentimes, believers put God in a box that limits Him to what they can comprehend. God does not have the same limitations that you have.

If you are currently in debt, you are probably feeling overwhelmed, stressed, and worried like we felt when we were over our heads in debt. God is able to do immeasurably more than anything that you could ask or imagine. The sky is the limit as far as He is concerned. He knows no earthly barriers or boundaries that will keep Him from fulfilling the best plans and purposes for your life. Have you ever experienced a debt being turned over to a debt collector? If so, you know that you will start getting those embarrassing repeated collection calls all day at work, home or on your cell phone until you pay or make arrangements. While it is easier to simply ignore creditors, you may never know how they can help to get your finances back on track. *Stay in constant communication with your creditors.* Don't be afraid to let them know about your financial situation. Use the debt stacking method chart located in the appendix to set up your strategic financial plan and start working your plan with expectancy. God has the power to do more than you can imagine.

Prayer:

Today, Lord, I am praying for a debt free life that is free from stress, worry, and frustration. Give me the resources that I need to put me in a position to payoff my outstanding debts so I can have more available resources to help build wealth. Amen.

Reading:

Ephesians 3:20: "Now to him who is able to do immeasurably more than all we ask or imagine, according to his power that is at work within us."

Application:

List your specific debts that you desire to be smaller:

DAY 7
Storing Up Treasures

Most potters create beautiful pieces of art out of clay jars. They take raw clay, shape and mold it to a specific shape, and then bake the clay until it becomes hard. Then they paint it, glaze it, and/or decorate the jars to be used for everyday use or decorations. In the biblical days, valuable documents were rolled up and placed inside a jar of clay and then hidden for safe keeping. As believers, God has made a way for us to be made new in this financial journey. He entrusts us to be responsible managers of His resources. A part of being a responsible manager is safeguarding our financial future. In 2 Corinthians 4:7, Paul summarizes that God gives His power to men, so that His power might be made perfect in human weakness. We are God's vessel here for a purpose, to share His treasures. "Treasures" can be our testimonies, sharing the Gospel, love, our knowledge, etc.

Even through the stress of our financial difficulties, God is shaping and molding us for the journey. "Life happens" is a popular urban saying that means that no matter how much a person plans, no one can predict the future, so you must choose to make the best of it. Life involves so many risks that could potentially cause loss or damage. Some risks are predictable and other risks are unpredictable. When we learned that our daughter, Kennedi was born severely brain injured and would never walk, talk, or eat on her our own, it was major blow! Nothing could have prepared us for this type of tragedy. Not even the money that we had saved for a rainy day. As we mentioned before, her illness and subsequent death limited our ability to earn enough money to take care of all of her unexpected medical and funeral expenses. We were wiped out of every dime we had. Oftentimes we felt so weak, but God gave us power to endure in the midst of our weakness.

We thank God that we had medical, dental insurance, and a small savings to cover some of Kennedi's medical and dental expenses. We were so overwhelmed, we did not take the time to think about and plan for the risk of actually losing Kennedi to death. Therefore, I failed to select the life-insurance supplement option for her and our sons on my employee health plan. Not having life and burial insurance for Kennedi put us in another financial dilemma. We will cover life insurance more in depth later. We learned many life lessons from that experience. We learned that safeguarding our financial future was just as important as managing our finances. Being a good financial manager includes being a risk manager. There are four stages of risk management: (1) risk avoidance, (2) risk reduction, (3) risk retention, and (4) risk transfer. Purchasing insurance is one of the most effective ways of transferring risk. (Florida Insurance Licensing - American Safely Council, Inc. 2013)

You must learn how to avoid as many risks as possible. You can reduce risks by taking the necessary precautions to protect yourself and your family. Your retention is making an assessment of your risk factors and making financial preparation for possible loss. Then you must transfer your risk to an insurance company. Make sure you have insurance protection. The purpose of insurance is to provide protection against specific types of financial loss. Choose your insurance carefully by assessing your potential risks and your specific needs. Insurance coverage varies with every individual and family. Shop around for the best coverage at the best prices. We suggest that you get the following five types of basic insurance coverage: (1) automobile insurance, (2) health insurance, (3) disability insurance, (4) homeowners or renters insurance, and (5) life insurance. There will be times when you will feel the blows of life that leave you feeling weak and powerless, but lean on God!

Prayer:

Today, Lord, shape me, mold me, and stretch me like clay so that I may be equipped for the financial journey that lies ahead of me. Even though I face risks every day of my life, I know that You are protecting from all hurt, harm, and danger. Amen.

Reading:

2 Corinthians 4:7" "But we have this treasure in jars of clay to show that this all-surpassing power is from God and not from us."

Application:

Make an assessment of your potential risks. List your specific insurance needs.

DAY 8
True Treasures of the Heart

We are pouring out our hearts to you in this book because we know that we are living in days wherein people are seeking truth and transparency. Just like we were brokenhearted by the tragic illness and death of our only daughter, Kennedi, many people are just as brokenhearted because someone has left them, has died, has deceived them, or disappointed them. It was only by God's power of healing that mended our broken hearts so that we could truly experience a financial renewal. We know the feeling all too well how a broken heart can be debilitating as you keep reliving the hurt and painful memories over and over again. If you do not get delivered, your hurt will be the driving force of your life. It will be like cancer; it will grow and spread until it affects every aspect of your life. No matter what you do or say, people will see your broken heart.

We can share with you all of these great biblical and financial principles, but you have to be willing to put your heart in it in order to experience the manifestation of God's power. Your heart tells it all. If your heart is not into something you will not give 100 percent of yourself to it. You might have good intentions, but it will suck the life out of you to succeed when you do something halfheartedly. In fact, most of the time you will find it emotionally draining to achieve your highest potential, which is why it is so easy for us to quit certain things. Our hearts simply were not in it. We treasure (value) whatever is in our heart. It could be our relationship with God or others, a job, a career, a book, material possessions, associations, ministry, etc. In Matthew 6:21, Jesus tells us that our desire and hope is tied to our treasure. He says, "For where your treasure is, there your heart will be also." Jesus tells the disciples that God, not possessions must be the center of their lives. If not, their good behavior will not suffice for it. Jesus knew whatever a disciple values will reveal where His treasure is.

You cannot hide where true loyalty lies. It will show whether you serve God or your possessions. Many Christians believe that they can have treasure on earth and in heaven, but there is only one true treasure, and that is God. God should always be at the center of your heart. Where is your treasure? Your treasure is what you believe is important and desirable. It influences the way you live, think, make decisions, your actions, your behavior, even how you manage your money. Putting God at the center of your heart connects your heart with His heart. It will cause you to chase after godly things rather than earthly things. It is impossible to serve God and man. In other words, your money and your heart go hand and hand. Whatever is at the center of your heart drives your life. Ken and I are surrounded by all types of people who are seeking happiness in things like money, social media, politics, and pleasures, only to find that none of these earthly things bring about the true peace of God.

Identifying your treasure will give you a sense of control of your financial destiny. We are not saying that you are not supposed to enjoy earthly things; we are simply saying *prioritize*. Make sure God is your first priority. Know what is important and what is not important. If being a good steward is ranked high on your list of priorities, you will set goals to please God in the area of stewardship. You will be motivated to start saving and spending according to your financial plan. When you put God at the center of life, you can experience the manifestation of God in your life and finances. Everything will divinely line up with His anointing—your finances, your ministry, your job, your marriage, your children, your friendships, etc. On the flip side, if you replace God with earthly pleasures such as money, material things, people, and places, everything in your life is driven by that thing, or things, that have replaced God. For an example, if money is at the center of your life, your relationships will be driven by money, your job will be driven by money, and your children will be driven by money. Your focus will become materialist. God says, "You shall have no other gods before me" (Exodus 20:3). Putting God at the center of your heart will allow you to experience the power of God in every area of your life.

Prayer:

Today, Lord, I thank You for all Your treasures. Help me to remember where my true treasure is and to keep my heart right about my possessions. Amen.

Reading:

Matthew 6:21: "For where your treasure is, there your heart will be also."

Application:

Make a list of everything that is important to you and put them in order by priority. How can you put God's kingdom agenda at the center of your heart?

DAY 9
Serving a Miracle-Working God

A miracle is an event that would be impossible by natural law but is brought to pass by the supernatural power of God. God has performed so many miracles in our personal finances from 2003, when our daughter, Kennedi, was born, until today. We serve a miracle-working God. We have heard and read about so many miracles that God performed in the Bible. In Exodus 16:12–15, 31–35, God provided manna as food for Israel for forty years as they traveled to Canaan. This made a believer out of the Israelite. In Psalm 77:14, the psalmist speaks of the greatness of God. He describes a power that is beyond our understanding, a supernatural power that man cannot emulate.

It is important for you to understand that some financial blessings will happen supernaturally because of your faithfulness and obedience. God will perform miracles that will supersede your credit score, the money in your bank account, even rejections or denials. Your faith and prayer is the key to your financial miracles. God can perform miracles that you cannot explain in words, nor grasp with your mind. He can make the impossible possible. God proved His power of working miracles through Jesus's crucifixion and resurrection. "What no eye has seen, what no ear has heard, and what no human mind has conceived the things God has prepared for those who love Him" (1 Corinthians 2:9).

When we were looking to buy our first home, we were denied so many times that we almost believed some of the feedback from the bankers and loan officers. Some laughed in our faces. Some never called us back. Some told us it would take us at least ten years to buy a home. Some told us that we would never qualify for a home. Some told us that we needed perfect credit scores. Some asked for astronomical money up front. Some treated us like we were second-class citizens. However, we kept the faith and kept praying for God to work a miracle, and He did just that. God connected us with the right people at the right time. And no, we did not have perfect credit when we purchased our home, we had a perfect God.

God will strategically put people in place to work His miracles. We witnessed this with our bankers. I have always enjoyed the convenience of going through the drive-thru for most of my banking transactions. Ken, on the other hand, insists on walking in the branch so that he can build relationships with the bankers. He is a firm believer that when you build relationships with bankers, it builds trust. Ken feels that bankers are more susceptible to help you when you have developed a strong banking relationship with them. We have found this to be true. Every week we intentionally go in the bank, shake hands, and have small talk with the bankers at our local bank. As our relationships grew stronger, we noticed that the bankers began to give us special privileges such as the best interest rates, fee waivers or refunds, and other perks. We have been approved for loans when we were not creditworthy according to the standard bank-loan criteria. This is what it means to serve a miracle-working God.

In opening checking accounts, customers create several

legal relationships between themselves and the banks – often without being fully aware of the implications of any of them. First, the bank asks a new customer to sign a signature card, which is then kept on file so that the bank has some records of what the customer's authorized signature looks like. Second, the signature card creates an agency relationship. The third relationship is that of *debtor* and *creditor*. Assuming the customer or depositor has a positive balance in the checking account, the customer is a creditor of the bank, and the bank is a debtor of the customer. (Hiscox, Spandel and Lewis 2004)

You, like so many people, are in need of a financial miracle. If God did it for the Israelites and for our family, He can certainly do it for you. I am sure you can name several miracles that God has already performed in your life. Do not wait until you have a financial crisis to believe God for a miracle. Start thanking and praising Him now for what He has already done and for what He is about to do in your life. He is already touching, changing, and transforming your finances during this time of financial renewal. He is getting ready to "loose" anything that has been holding you down or holding you back. (Matthew 18:18) God is about to visit you with great power and anointing, giving you new clarity and wisdom as it relates to your finances.

Prayer:

Today, Lord, You know my current financial situation and what I have available to spend. I know You are a miracle-working God who has already made provisions for me even when I have been discredited, denied, and doubted by others. Make a financial miracle today. I claim your miracles and blessings. Amen.

Reading:

Psalm 77:14: "You are the God who performs miracles; you display your power among the peoples."

Application:

God performs miracles every day. If He did it for someone else, He can certainly do it for you! List a miracle that you need from God today.

DAY 10
Breaking the Financial Curse

Not hearing God's voice and obeying His Word is one of the reasons for financial curses. Proverbs 26:2 says a curse is "like a fluttering sparrow or a darting swallow, an undeserved curse does not come to rest." When the Israelites disobeyed God they paid the penalty by being caged into a wilderness for forty years. They received manna just to keep them alive while paying for their sin. The same happens to us when we disobey his principles. He leaves us to survive on manna that is just enough to get by and scarce enough to continue looking forward to being free from such mere survival. (Gondwe 2008) We believe financial curses are spiritual slavery that can be passed down from one generation to the next generation until the curse is broken. Children learn from their parents and guardians. If you saw your parents mismanage their money, chances are you will mismanage your money, your children will pick up similar bad habits, and then pass it on to their children. It is a never-ending saga. We are convinced that is why so many parents are raising a culture of materialistic children who lack the true understanding of financial literacy. Their only reference is what they have seen and been taught.

As I speak and teach on financial literacy, I typically start out by explaining what it means to mismanage money. The formal definition of mismanagement of money is to mishandle money in a way that negatively affects the financial standing of an individual. In other words, to mismanage money means you do not save money, you constantly overcharge your credit cards, you do not give, you do not live on a budget, you constantly overspend, and you live beyond your means. I have met many people, young and old, who did not know they were mismanaging their money until after I spoke on the topic. They admitted to managing their money the same way their parents or guardians managed it. I explained to them that this is a form of learned behavior that is based on what they were taught or what they had seen in the past. Poverty is listed as one of the curses and prosperity is listed as one of the seven blessings in Deuteronomy 28. Just like poverty is passed down generations, so is wealth. Most wealthy families pass down their wealth to multiple generations. We believe that is why the rich continue to get richer and the poor get poorer.

Financial curses can be broken in the name of Jesus. If you are in a financial curse, the Bible says the curse can be broken. When you accept Jesus as your savior, you can be free from demonic oppression that keep you in bondage. The Sovereignty of Jesus Christ gives us authority over the devil and his curses (Luke 9:1). The devil uses darkness to keep us blinded to God's truth. God's Word gives us light and understanding. Psalm 119:130 says, "The unfolding of your words gives light; it gives understanding to the simple. If you find that everyone in your family is experiencing major financial problems, chances are you are a part of a generational curse. Your family will continue to have financial difficulties until the curse is broken.

Malachi 3:9 places a curse on those Hebrews who did not tithe. The Lord felt that the Israelites had robbed God by withholding their tithes and offerings. God calls it robbery because they had possessions that belonged to Him. God commands us to give Him 10 percent tithes and offerings because it belongs to Him. He requires us to give Him 10 percent of our income, and He expects for us to manage the remaining 90 percent. When God's people did not give as He commanded, they were cursed with a curse. Once you recognize that there is a curse over your finances or your family's finances, you must put light on it by studying and meditating on God's Word. Ask God to use you to break the financial curse so you can pass down wealth instead of poverty.

Prayer:

Today, Lord, I bind every curse that has hindered my finances and been passed down from one generation to the next. Use me to break any curses that may be robbing me of the many blessings that You have in store for me. I command the spirit of poverty to leave me and my family, in the name of Jesus. Amen.

Reading:

Malachi 3:8–10. "Will a mere mortal rob God? Yet you rob me. "But you ask, 'How are we robbing you? "In tithes and offerings. You are under a curse—your whole nation—because you are robbing me. Bring the whole tithe into the storehouse, that there may be food in my house. Test me in this," says the Lord Almighty, "and see if I will not throw open the floodgates of heaven and pour out so much blessing that there will not be room enough to store it."

Application:

Our God is a jealous God. One of His commandments tell us "to have no other god before Him." What "gods" have been a hindrance to your financial renewal?

PART II
Renewing My Spirit

*Create in me a pure heart, O God, and
renew a steadfast spirit within me.*
—Psalm 51:10

DAY 11
Putting Faith in Action

Sadly, we have met a lot of Christians who do not believe in tithing. They have a misunderstanding and misperception about tithing. They may sing in their church choir, usher, or work in other church auxiliaries, but they are not comfortable with giving 10 percent of their tithes or offerings. Interestingly, most of the time, these are the people who do the most complaining in the church or the ones who are always unhappy with the leadership of the church. As mentioned before, a lot of this comes from what has been passed down from generation to generation. We are living in days wherein contributions to churches and other religious groups are at a decline because people are living more self-centered lives opposed to God-centered lives.

As church leaders, we have seen and heard it all as it relates to tithing and offerings. We have heard "I am not going to give because my money will go to the pastor so he can get him a new Mercedes Benz," "I am not going to give because my tithes and offerings are going into the pastor's personal bank account," or "I am not going to give my tithes so that the pastor's wife can buy new clothes and church hats." We have heard enough misconceptions on this topic that we could literally write another book on all the misconceptions about church giving. Giving to God and others is a faith walk. Hebrews 11:1 says, "Now faith is confidence in what we hope for and assurance about what we do not see." This scripture encourages believers to grow and remain steadfast in our faith. Faith in God is the foundation of our relationship with Him and serves as a necessity for the Christian life. Faith requires you to live a life that trusts in God's promises in spite of your situation and circumstances. You must have faith that your contribution to your local church belongs to God. Faith in God is the foundation of our relationship with Him. When you release your contribution to God by faith, you are putting your faith into action.

Oftentimes, people in the Body of Christ forget that many pastors are on a regular salary just like they are. As a matter of fact, the average salary for a Methodist pastor is $27,880 to $49,200 (Salary Genius). That means that pastors and their families have to manage their money and pay bills just like everyone else in the church. When we go to the bank to get a loan, they do not extend credit based on the church's credit history or what is in the church's bank account. Lenders have to look at our debt-to-income (DTI) ratio when deciding whether or not to lend us money or extend credit. If we have a low DTI, there is a greater chance for us to get approved for a loan or credit. If it is too high, we will not be extended a loan just like anyone else. Banks generally want to see your DTI below 30 before they will approve a loan.

Your DTI is a number that expresses the relationship between your total monthly debt and your gross monthly income. The formula for DTI is total monthly debt payments divided by monthly income. Say you pay $1,350 a month for rent, $450 a month for your car loan, $170 a month for credit cards (Total is $1,970), and your gross monthly income is $6,500.

Your gross monthly income is the money you earn before taxes and deductions. You would add up all of your monthly debt payments of $1,970 and divide it by your gross monthly income of $6,500 to get your DTI of 30% ($1,9700 / $6,500 = 30%). Based on my finance background, I typically calculate our monthly income allocation (MIA) before we apply for loans to see if we are budgetarily ready for a loan. You should do the same. Use the monthly income allocation form to calculate your DTI. This form is located in the appendix at the back of this book.

Many pastors make below-average salaries at their churches, so they have to be bi-vocational - work a second job to provide for their families. Some people view pastors and their families as glamorous as in some of the reality TV shows. Those shows are depicting the lifestyle of megachurches, which are the churches that have weekly attendance of two thousand persons or more in their worship services. There is only about fifty megachurches in the United States. The rest of us are seeing small to medium size congregations. In fact, the average size church in America is seeing about ninety people.

With all of the negative publicity surrounding pastors and money, it takes faith in God to understand that you are giving unto God and not man. He will protect the Body of Christ and expose any misappropriation of money. Hebrews 11:1 tells us what real faith is—the response to God's will and Word. Faith is accepting something simply because God said it. Faith is a covenant between you and God. God did not intend for your tithes and offerings to cause a burden on your life. You should be giving as an honor and a privilege. It should be out of your love for God and your desire to help build His kingdom.

Prayer:

Today, Lord, I don't have as much money as I desire. But by faith I will honor You with what I have. I pray that You will be honored greatly this day as I give to You what already belongs to You. Amen.

Reading:

Hebrews 11:1: "Now faith is confidence in what we hope for and assurance about what we do not see."

Application:

How has your faith increased your giving?

DAY 12
It Shall Be Done if You Believe

While working on my undergraduate degree at Dallas Baptist University, I was required to take a Fine Arts class. One of my assignments was to critique an artist's work. I studied the artist for several weeks before I was ready to critic his artwork. I learned the artist starts drawing with the end result in mind. Artists already know what the completed work will look like. They very seldom start painting or drawing without a plan or vision. Artists oftentimes have to separate what they see from what they perceive when they paint a picture. When you create a financial plan, like an artist, you are painting your financial future. You cannot get distracted by your current financial situation—struggling to pay your monthly bills, little or no savings, and lack of money. You must separate what you see in your financial future from what you see now so you can experience financial renewal.

Your belief system changes your vision. When you believe in God's word, you will see so many possibilities in your finances. In Matthew 21:21, when the disciples saw the fig tree wither, they asked Jesus, "How did the fig tree wither at once?" In other words, they were asking how can Israel so quickly perish as God's people? Jesus replies that the new kingdom of God has come in Jesus and in those who have faith in Jesus.

Those who are able to "move mountains" in fulfilling their calling will be able to produce the fruits of the kingdom. It takes drive, determination, and passion to "move mountains" in your life. You may feel like your current financial situation is like a big "mountain." We are reminded of an oldie but goodie gospel song by Inez Andrews that says, "Now Lord don't move my mountain but give me the strength to climb, and Lord, don't take away my stumbling blocks but lead me all around." God may not move your "mountain" of financial struggles, but know that He will give you strength and lead you through the process of building your financial future. You have to separate what you see from what you perceive and place your faith in God's almighty power.

As your financial perspectives and prerogatives begin to line up with God's word, you will be able to "move mountains". To "move mountains" is having faith to do something that seems impossible. At my graduation commencement service at Dallas Baptist University in May 2004, Dr. Sheila Bailey, our commencement speaker and wife of the late Dr. E. K. Bailey, who founded and pastored Concord Baptist Church in Dallas for many years, quoted her husband's definition of faith: "acting like something is so, even when it is not so, in order that it might be so, simply because God said so." The bottom line, is that it shall be done if you believe. God already knows how much money you have and how much you need. As you follow God, you will find yourself prospering while others are struggling financially and walking in spiritual darkness. Your belief system allows you to see where you are going and how you will get there. You must see financial victory in your mind first, then your finances will match up with what you see and what you see will produce the fruits of the kingdom.

Prayer:

Today, Lord, I believe I can accomplish anything through You because You give me strength and confidence to overcome any obstacles that come my way. Prepare me emotionally, financially, mentally, and spiritually for a financial renewal. Amen.

Reading:

Matthew 21:21: "Jesus replied, 'Truly I tell you, if you have faith and do not doubt, not only can you do what was done to the fig tree, but also you can say to this mountain, "Go, throw yourself into the sea," and it will be done.'"

Application:

List all doubts that you will surrender to God today.

DAY 13
Being Content

Today you will uncover the secrets of true contentment when it comes to your finances and your material possessions. You will have the opportunity to examine your heart, thoughts, and attitude about your finances. Our prayer is to give you some truths about being content in your life. We live in a society that teaches us that contentment is tied to our ability to constantly acquire more. Our basic value is that more is better. More education, more money, more houses, more cars, more clothes, more shoes, the list goes on and on. Most people often say that they will finally be content if they get more of—you can fill in the blank. There is a never-ending saga of people in our society wanting more, which leads to a generation of discontented people. It is important that you grasp the difference between your needs and your wants.

In 1 Timothy 6:6–7, the apostle Paul instructed and advised Timothy to do what he could as a pastor to stop the negative ties to riches in the church. The church at Ephesus had become blindly arrogant because of their riches and allowed what they owned to become their primary source for life. He reminded the church that every earthly possession is only meant for this life on earth. As believers, we entered this world with nothing, and we will leave this world with nothing. Godliness is the greatest gain. A godly person should be content with what they have because they have much more than they had when they came into the world. Therefore, Apostle Paul encourages us to fight arrogance daily, put our hope in God, and not in money or other material possessions. As you can see, the same types of behavior continue today.

Since your needs and wants are unlimited, you are always going to need more and want more. So many businesses respond to your unlimited needs and wants and uses it to make a profit. In order for any business to be profitable, the company must understand their customers. They pay markers to study consumer behavior so they know exactly how to market us to buy their products. Advertisers in particular understand that people have different perspectives of what contentment means. Accordingly, they spend billions of dollars on innovative and creative advertisements that create customer needs. Many people define contentment as material gains such as money, a great career, a house, cars, name brand purses and shoes, jewelry, etc. However, true contentment is the state of being satisfied with what you already have. What may be satisfactory to you may not be satisfactory to others.

We live in such a highly technological society that there are ways to measure what we are purchasing as consumers. The Nielsen company studies consumer behavior from one hundred countries to give a complete view of trends and habits worldwide. (Nielsen: About Us 2017)They analyze what we as consumers are buying on a regular basis from our food, clothes, shoes, books, smart phones, cars, and much more. Based on their analysis, Americans are big spenders. If you are like most consumers, sometimes you buy things without thinking about your financial plan and goals. Notice how as soon as you buy a new cell phone, there is a new one coming out on the market shortly thereafter. You naturally find yourself compelled to buy the latest, greatest cell phone. Again, it's never ending. When you spend like this regularly, it can consume a large portion of your money.

God desires you to be content. His Word tells you that you must be content in all things: "Keep your lives free from the love of money and be content with what you have, because God has said, 'Never will I leave you; never will I forsake you.'" (Hebrews 13:5) But because of your human desires, you may find that the things of the this world to can blind you and keep you from seeing God's specific instructions as it relates to being content in your daily living. Learn to be content with what you have. Stick to your budget plan so you can control your spending and stay within your means.

Prayer:

Today, Lord, grant me true contentment. Help me to accept what today brings, to be satisfied with what I have and who I am. Give me peace in the midst of my storms. Amen.

Reading:

1 Timothy 6:6–7: "But godliness with contentment is great gain. For we brought nothing into the world, and we can take nothing out of it."

Application:

What do you think God wants you to learn from your present financial circumstances?

DAY 14
Touch and Agree

There is so much power in touching and agreeing with one another in the name of Jesus. To be in agreement is to be in unity, and to have the same vision. To touch and agree is when you stand as one with someone. Every person involved must be on one accord. It is very difficult to touch and agree with someone with a different vision than you. Communication is the key. You must be willing to be open and transparent with each other in order to touch and agree. Otherwise, you could possibly be touching and not agreeing, which is defeating the purpose.

As mentioned, we have faced all types of situations and circumstances in our marriage. Statistically, we should have divorced a long time ago. However, we intentionally make time to discuss our finances, and come to a mutual agreement on how we desire God to help us get through our struggles. It is easy to go into panic mode and start playing the blame game when you are having financial struggles. We have certainly witnessed a large number of divorces in the Body of Christ. Most of the time it's due to poor communication and disagreements in the marriage. There is a legal term in divorce court for couples who can't come to agreement called "irreconcilable differences". This means that the couples believe there is no hope for working out their disagreements.

We touch and agree on our finances, new purchases, family decisions, and any other major life decisions because we realize financial struggles can ruin relationships. We especially understand the importance of communicating about all major purchases with other. Money can ruin friendships and destroy families if you have to borrow and are unable to pay it back on the agreed date. It can ruin a marriage when you are constantly fighting about it. The "fight" is typically about how money should or should not be spent. When considering a Christian marriage, you must ask the hard, but necessary questions before making a lifetime commitment.

There are two main questions that you must agree on if you plan on being together for a long time. Who does my money belong to? How do I manage my money? If you do not agree on the answers to these questions before marriage, you surely will not be in agreement after you marry. Financial problems is one of the top causes of divorce. Make sure that you both agree that God owns everything, including your money, and that you are stewards of the resources that God has entrusted you with.

It is important that you and your spouse or significant other have the same worldview and biblical view about money. Your worldview is how you view reality, make sense of life and the world. It serves as the necessary foundation for your thoughts and actions. Your biblical worldview is based on how you view the world through the lens of Bible truths. It serves as the necessary foundation for how you treat others and live your life each day. If both of you don't have the same belief system, it will cause major confusion and a great deal of arguments in the relationship. The Bible defines this as being unequally yoked in 2 Corinthians 6:14: "Do not be yoked together with unbelievers. For what do righteousness and wickedness have in common? Or what fellowship can light have with darkness?" If your significant other, doesn't agree with your worldview and biblical views, don't try to force your beliefs on him or her. This is your opportunity to allow God to connect you with someone else who you are equally yoked in a relationship.

Many people grow up with little or no training on how to manage money. Therefore, they are forced to rely on worldly influences such as the media, social media, and Reality TV to teach them on how to manages their money. As a result, they lack the ability to set priorities. In my financial literacy workshops, I have met many people who lack the basic discipline needed to set and keep a budget. I share the importance of learning how to budget before they combine their finances in a relationship. In Matthew 18:19, Jesus says, "Again, I tell you that if two of you on earth agree about anything you ask for, it will be done for you by my Father in heaven." Jesus is teaching us to come together with one another in our prayer lives.

Prayer gives you power to accept what God wants to achieve through you. He wants you to unite with other believers so that you can receive His blessings and favor. People often misunderstand what it takes to merge two lives together in marriage under God. This is a time where you humble yourselves before God, putting your heart and mind on prayer, fasting, and waiting for directions from God. You must also understand that everyone has different spiritual gifts in the Body of Christ. Every part of the body has to function properly in order to be effective. Think about your own body. When you experience pain in a specific area of your body, oftentimes it affects other parts of the body. There is a supernatural power that takes place when there is an agreement in the form of a partnership with you, God, and others.

Prayer:

Today, Lord, I touch and agree with my brothers and sisters who are participating in this forty-day financial renewal experience with me. I am standing on your word and promises that have already been established in heaven for me. Amen.

Read:

Matthew 18:19. "Again, I tell you that if two of you on earth agree about anything you ask for, it will be done for you by my Father in heaven."

Application:

Pray with at least two people about your finances today. List their names and their prayer requests:

DAY 15
Being a Cheerful Giver

Giving is a lifestyle. God desires for us to give just as He gives to us. He looks forward to rewarding you when you give. In Mark 9:41, Jesus promises those who gave His followers a cup of water, He would reward them. The only expectation from Him is for you to be cheerful when you give. Many Christians do not give because they do not know what the Bible teaches about stewardship and giving. As leaders, we have an obligation to teach the Body of Christ in the area of giving. We are proud to be cheerful givers, especially after we saw what God does supernaturally with cheerful givers. That why we get ex cited when we give our tithes and offering unto God. We can both literally say that we have never seen God forsake us when it comes to our personal finances. Ever since we agreed that we would not rob God no matter how bad things get with our finances, we have received so many blessings from God. Every time we get blessed, we look forward to blessing others. In 2 Corinthians 9:7, Paul encouraged the Corinthian Christians to support the needs of the believers in Judea. He wrote, "Let each one do just as he has resolved in his heart, not grudgingly or under compulsion, for God loves a cheerful giver."

Paul specifically tells believers that their giving should not be reluctant and forced. During that time, the Corinthians were struggling with unity, which had caused a delay in their giving. There is nothing worse than a person who gives begrudgingly. We have experienced people in the church who will give to a special event or occasion, but they complain or are angry when they give. Some refuse to give because of their personal issues. Not only does it hurt those who witness this type of behavior, but it hurts the person who is giving out of reluctance or refuses to give. The Word says they will not prosper. A reluctant giver feels like giving is a chore, an obligation, forced or coerced. I do not know anyone who wants to receive a gift from a reluctant giver. Most of us would rather receive a gift from someone who looks forward to giving, who gives out of the kindness of their hearts or simply because they enjoy helping others.

Being a giver is a part of stewardship. If you are not a giver, pray about it. It's not too late for you to learn how to give now. You don't have to wait until you make more money or get extra money. Make a choice to commit to giving a certain amount. It could be weekly, monthly, yearly, or random. A good place to start is by giving in increments – you can start out with 3%, increase to 5%, increase to 10%, increase to 13%, continue to increase to your comfort. This may seem like a lot in the beginning, but if you make is a part of your budget or set it up as an automatic bank draft, you won't think about it as much. When you give, not only can you take advantage of the tax deductions credit for charitable donations, but you can also expect blessings. Your blessings may not come exactly when you want them, but they are always right on time. God will send a blessing when you least expect it. His desire is for you to prosper (Psalm 35:27). The more you give, the more He blesses you.

Show us a person who is a cheerful giver, and we will show

you a prosperous individual. Show us a person who never gives or gives reluctantly, and we will show you a person who constantly lives in a state of lack. Those are the people who constantly complain about never having enough money. You can learn to be a cheerful giver by studying the greatest giver ever known on earth, Jesus Christ. He gave up His own life so that we could have everlasting life. Jesus told us, "It is more blessed to give than to receive" (Acts 20:35). Our motivation for being a "cheerful giver" should be that it pleases the Lord and reflects His gift of salvation. God wants you to give Him your time, energy, money, and other material possessions. You should do it out of the kindness of your heart, not expecting anything in return. This type of giving will not only bless others, but it blesses God because He "loves a cheerful giver."

Prayer:

Today, Lord, Thank You for the sacrificing Your life for me so that I can have eternal life. I will give cheerfully, not grudgingly or because I am made to knowing that You love a cheerful giver. Amen.

Read:

2 Corinthians 9:7: "Each of you should give what you have decided in your heart to give, not reluctantly or under compulsion, for God loves a cheerful giver."

Application.

What are your thoughts about being a cheerful giver? List ways that you can be more of a cheerful giver.

DAY 16
Being a Generous Giver

Christians should be engaged in sharing with one another—so "there are no needy among them" (Acts 4:34). Such sharing promotes a radical generosity. The only way you can be a generous giver is by understanding your role as a steward. Psalm 24:1: "The earth is the Lord's, and everything in it, the world, and all who live in it." Your mind-set about money has to line up with God's Word. There are different levels of giving. By now you know what it means to be a cheerful giver; now you need to understand how to be a generous giver. First, allow us to explain a generous giver. A generous giver gives not only cheerfully, but they give extravagantly without limits.

Most generous givers give to their local church first. They understand that giving to their local church keeps them spiritually grounded, well balanced, and sensitive to the needs of the church and people. They consistently give to their local church out of their love for the church and for their passion to support the works of evangelism, Christian education, missions, and other ministries within the local church and community. They realize that their giving contributes to kingdom building and their generosity provides stability to their church. Generous givers do not worry about how the church will spend the money that they have given; rather, they trust that God will cover them and their church. As they grow in their giving, they typically seek ways to give generously outside of their local church.

Givers give, expecting God to bless them even more. God is able to bless you abundantly so that in all things at all times, you will have all that you need (2 Corinthians 9:8). Paul demonstrates this in 1 Timothy 6:18 when he addresses the believers who are rich. He instructs them not to be conceited or to fix their hope on the uncertainty of riches, but on God. God is the one who supplies us with all things to enjoy, and He expects us to be generous and willing to share it with others. I am reminded of our annual travel to Fort Valley, Georgia, to visit Ken's family. Every time we go, we are blessed by our family and friends. We always make our way to Lane Southern Orchards to get delicious fresh bottles of peach cider and carts of juicy peaches.

"Lane Southern Orchards has been planting, growing, and harvesting the best-tasting peaches and pecans in Georgia since 1908." [2] Every year we look forward to buying cases of bottles of peach cider and peaches to give to our friends and family in Texas. We give to members of our church. I look forward to giving my coworkers fresh bottles of peach cider for the holidays. One of the responses that I get from my coworkers when I give is, "Thank you for being so generous." It's a powerful feeling to be a blessing to someone else's life. God is a giver. When you are a generous giver, you are becoming like Him.

Ken and I always look for opportunities to bless others. You should give to others knowing that God is so generous in

---

[2] 2013. *Lane Southern Orchards.* http://www.lanesouthernorchards.com/about-us.

supplying all of your needs. As you grow to becoming a generous giver, consider adding charitable giving as a regular expense in your budget. Choose a charity that you are passionate about. We have a strong interest in children with special needs, and therefore we look for opportunities to give to specific organizations that aids children with special needs. There are a lot of scams, so be careful when choosing a new organization to give to. We often use an organization called Charity Navigator to research new or unfamiliar organizations. You can go to www.charitynavigator.org to get a detailed report about any organization that you are interested in. Be sure to keep all of your receipts so you can use your contributions as a tax deduction.

There are many generous Christians who support the church and charities, but they are small in number compared to all of the people in need. If only everyone would do their part in the Body of Christ, there would be more ministries to help people. God will reward generous givers with spiritual blessings now and eternally. As you grow in your giving, you will start thinking of ways to give even more.

Prayer:

Today, Lord, You have been so generous to me when You gave me another opportunity to see this day that wasn't promised to me. I realize there were many people who did not have an opportunity to see this day. I am grateful for Your grace and mercy. Continue to increase my faith and finance. Amen.

Read:

1 Timothy 6:18: "Command them to do good, to be rich in good deeds, and to be generous and willing to share."

Application:

Think about the goodness of Jesus and all that He has blessed you with (i.e., clothes, shoes, foods, furniture, money, etc.). What are you willing to donate to charity or goodwill today?

DAY 17
Trusting God for a Financial Breakthrough

You may be reading this book during a major financial crisis or you may be a little behind with your bills. Whatever the case, you need to trust God for a financial breakthrough. It may seem like you can never get ahead because you find yourself constantly robbing Peter to pay Paul most of the time. We truly understand what it is like to desperately be in need of a financial breakthrough. We were determined not to allow the financial pressures to take control of our lives. Clearly, the Lord had already spoken to us through His Word. Every day we would recite Psalm 46:1–5:

> *God is our refuge and strength, an ever-present help in trouble. Therefore, we will not fear, though the earth give way and the mountains fall into the heart of the sea, though its waters roar and foam and the mountains quake with their surging. God is within her, she will not fall; God will help her at break of day.*

A financial breakthrough is when you are patiently waiting for a divine intervention that will help you to overcome your financial situation. You must seek God and make your request know to Him in prayer. You must P.U.S.H. - pray until something happens. In other words, you must move forward against obstacles that you face. The Holy Spirit will give you strength to push against your financial difficulties, your doubt, and your fears if trust God. Have faith that He will supply all of your needs according to His riches in glory through Christ Jesus. (Romans 8:32) No one likes experiencing financial hardships. It is especially hard to swallow when you feel like you are trying your best to live according to God's biblical principles, yet you see others who are prospering but living a seemingly worldly life. You may find yourself experiencing some envy. There is no need to envy them because God will bless you if you remain faithful to His Word.

The enemy tends to prey on our desperation and vulnerabilities. That is why he uses many get-rich-quick schemes to take advantage of those who come across desperate for money in the Body of Christ. Proverb 28:20 is a warning to leaders who were leading their people in an evil way. It clearly proves that when you are faithful to God, you will be rewarded. When man does not reward those who are faithful, the Lord will. Those who are eager to get rich will be punished. When you find yourself in a desperate state of mind, P.U.S.H. until your get your financial breakthrough!

We remember a time when we needed assistance with Kennedi's tuition to attend Our Children's Center, a daycare for children with special needs. If we did not come up with the funds, she would not be able to return. We remained faithful. One day the manager of the center informed us that we had received an anonymous partial scholarship for Kennedi's tuition, which allowed her to continue to attend for the rest of the year. That was a great blessing! We could go to work in peace knowing the staff understood her special needs, and therefore made appropriate accommodations to support her learning and development. That was a major financial breakthrough. God uses people like the anonymous donor to provide financial blessings and powerful testimonies to help open the door to His greatest financial breakthroughs.

The enemy will try to rob you of your sanity, joy, and hope. At this point, you know that this is not how God wants you to spend the rest of your life. God will do something miraculous with your finances when you trust Him. Just like God gave us strength through our pain, hardship, and setback, He will do the same for you. Trust God for a financial breakthrough.

Prayer:

Today, Lord, I know you want me to be financially whole, able to sufficiently provide for myself, my family, and my church. I am expecting a major financial breakthrough, and manifestations of your favor during this 40 days financial renewal experience. Amen.

Read:

Proverbs 28:20: "A faithful man will be richly blessed, but one eager to get rich will not go unpunished."

Application:

What financial breakthrough are you expecting from God today?

DAY 18
Investing Wisely

Unfortunately, there are not a lot of people who make financial investments in the Body of Christ. In fact, every time Ken and I have ever seen it introduced in the church, we notice some people's discomfort with investing. Some of the biggest misconceptions about investing is that investing is too risky and only for wealthy people. Despite these common misconceptions about investing, it is imperative that you research and learn more about investing. Investing is taking measures to make your money grow. It's when you buy stocks, properties, or anything that will increase value over a period of time. The following are the benefits of investing:

- Investing is a great way of making money
- The rewards of investing can last a lifetime
- Investing can help you beat inflation
- Investing is a way of owning a piece of corporate America

As you know, a lot of jobs are evolving and being replaced with technology. Those days are over when you work for one company until you retire. At this point, you have probably held many jobs in your life. If you are a young adult reading this book, chances are you will have many jobs in your lifetime. Thus, it is important that you start planning for your future while you are young.

Your long-term financial security is based on how you invest your money, so learn to invest wisely. As I travel to different conferences to speak about the importance of financial literacy, I often get asked, "When should I start investing?" My response is always the same. You should consider investing when you meet the following financial conditions:

- When you are able to pay all of our monthly expenses on time and still have money left over
- When you have paid off or lowered your major debts
- When you have adequate insurance coverage including life insurance
- When you have an emergency savings that covers at least six months of living expenses

Hopefully, you are putting at least 5–10 percent of your income in your savings account each month. You should set a goal to save up to $10,000 or at least six months of living expenses. Once you reach your saving goal, we suggest that you consider investing a portion of your money. Investing can be very confusing because there are different kinds of investments to choose from. The risks range from low to high. There are three main types of investments: stocks, bonds, and mutual funds. Stocks are owning a percentage of a corporation. When I teach about stocks in the classroom, I often use an example of an "apple pie" as a metaphor to illustrate buying stocks. When you buy stocks of a corporation that means that you are a stockholder, you have bought a piece of your favorite pie (business). You will have equity in the company and will share in the company's profits. Bonds are certificate of debt issued by a corporation or government.

When you buy a bond, that means you are lending money to the issuer of the bond. Mutual funds are created by pooling the money of many people and investing it in a collection of securities. If this is new information, praise God! That means you are learning and growing. If you are new to investing, we suggest that you start your first experience with investing within a 401(k) or similar employer- sponsored retirement plan and/ or *money market account*. Money market accounts are similar to an interest-bearing account, except they earn dividends instead of interest. They are low-risk, short-term securities and considered the safest investments. As you earn more income, you can take higher risks. To learn more about your investing opportunities, contact a financial advisor or talk to your employer benefits coordinator about employer-sponsored retirement programs.

You can find a lot of wisdom about investing in Matthew 25:14-28. It tells of a master who goes away and leaves a certain company to fulfill a task till he returns. This is one of the most powerful stories of investing, found in the parable of the talents found in Matthew 25:14-30:

> *"Again, the Kingdom of Heaven can be illustrated by the story of a man going on a long trip. He called together his servants and entrusted his money to them while he was gone. He gave five bags of silver[a] to one, two bags of silver to another, and one bag of silver to the last—dividing it in proportion to their abilities. He then left on his trip. The servant who received the five bags of silver began to invest the money and earned five more. The servant with*

two bags of silver also went to work and earned two more. But the servant who received the one bag of silver dug a hole in the ground and hid the master's money. After a long time their master returned from his trip and called them to give an account of how they had used his money. The servant to whom he had entrusted the five bags of silver came forward with five more and said, 'Master, you gave me five bags of silver to invest, and I have earned five more.'

The master was full of praise. 'Well done, my good and faithful servant. You have been faithful in handling this small amount, so now I will give you many more responsibilities. Let's celebrate together![b]' The servant who had received the two bags of silver came forward and said, 'Master, you gave me two bags of silver to invest, and I have earned two more.' The master said, 'Well done, my good and faithful servant. You have been faithful in handling this small amount, so now I will give you many more responsibilities. Let's celebrate together!' Then the servant with the one bag of silver came and said, 'Master, I knew you were a harsh man, harvesting crops you didn't plant and gathering crops you didn't cultivate. I was afraid I would lose your money, so I hid it in the earth.

Look, here is your money back.' But the master replied, 'You wicked and lazy servant! If you knew I harvested crops I didn't plant and gathered crops I didn't cultivate, why didn't you deposit my money in the bank? At least I could have gotten some interest on it.' Then he ordered, 'Take the money from this servant, and give it to the one with the ten bags *of silver. To those who use well what they are given, even more will be given, and they will have an abundance. But from those who do nothing, even what little they have will be taken away. Now throw this useless servant into outer darkness, where there will be weeping and gnashing of teeth.'"*

Buying a home is another type of investment. Owning a home is one of the largest financial assets in your investment portfolio. There are great benefits to buying your own home. You can deduct the cost of your mortgage loan interest and property taxes from your federal income taxes. Your home can appreciate and gain value over the years. It increases your net worth. There are two basic types of mortgages, fixed and adjustable rates. The interest rates for buying a home is one of the most important factors when choosing a mortgage. The lower the interest rate, the better the mortgage rates. When you rent from someone, you are helping them to build wealth. If you are not a home owner, consider meeting with a mortgage banker in the near future to discuss a plan for buying your first home. Making wise investments gives you the opportunity to accumulate wealth over time to meet your future financial needs and goals.

Prayer:

Today, Lord, give me wisdom and sound decisions to make investments that will create wealth for a lifetime. And give me the spirit of discernment to know how and when to diversify my investment portfolio. Amen.

Reading:

Matthew 25:14: "Again, the Kingdom of Heaven can be illustrated by the story of a man going on a long trip. He called together his servants and entrusted his money to them while he was gone."

Application:

When have you witnessed a return on an investment that involved you investing your time, talent, and treasure?

DAY 19
Seeking God First

There is a difference between being a customer and consumer. Customers buy products and consumers use products. We are all consumers, people who purchase and use goods and services on a daily basis. Our consumer behavior is driven by learned behavior. Many people tend to make poor choices when presented with the many options offered by the market economy. There are so many products and services to choose from. Some of the common reasons for poor choices is due to: a lack of planning, failure to use information, impulse buying, overspending, poor communication, and learned behavior. Yes, even how and why you choose your purchases are acquired behaviors. If poor consumer behaviors are not corrected, they will be passed on to the next generation. The youth around your life are watching you very closely. Not only are they watching how you spend your money, but they are also watching a lot of reality TV shows and learning how they spend their money.

They do not realize that some of the reality TV "shows" are not reality. They are intended to skew our perception of reality. Each person on the reality TV show has to be cast for their role, which means that there is some "acting" taking place to make a good TV show. It has to be entertaining with lots of drama. The more drama, the more ratings. Reality TV shows teaches us that everybody can be a celebrity. We are living in a society wherein many people are desperately seeking to be famous and competing to see who gets the most "views" and "likes" when they go live on social media. Many Christians are caught up in all the "lights, camera, and action" of their very own lives. Sometimes there is more drama going on in the church than the most popular, entertaining reality TV show. People are seeking for identity in worldly things and people. You must always seek God first for your identity.

How you spend our money is a reflection of your level of obedience toward God. The only order for your lives is God's divine order. His Word declares that "His thoughts are not our thoughts neither His ways our ways" (Isaiah 55:8). There have been so many times when we thought doing things our way was easier. Ken and I would execute a plan that we thought would work for us. Of course, the plan would always fail because we did not seek God first for guidance. We learned that even when we prepare a plan, the plan must line up with God's divine plan for our lives. In order to fulfill God's purpose, you have to keep God in His rightful place. He must be first place in your life as you seek first His kingdom and His righteousness according to Matthew 6:33. This scripture is from the great Sermon on the Mount. It tells Christians not to lay up for ourselves treasures upon the earth. Instead, you should seek God first in your daily walk. God is first should be first in your marriage, children, finances, ministry, etc.

Deuteronomy 6:5 tell us to "Love the Lord your God with all your heart and with all your soul and with all your strength." The world would have us think our lives are to be lived out thinking only about our selfish desires. Even in the midst of the worst crisis in our lives, we must remain steadfast.

There were times when we have gone to the church or a ministry event completely drained, tired, frustrated, and weak, but God would use us in a mighty way. We have learned in a very intimate way that His strength is made perfect in our weakness (2 Corinthians 12:9).

We thank God daily for purging us of selfishness, wrong priorities and wrong focus. Our daughter, Kennedi, really put a lot of things in perspective for us. In the mist of all the financial difficulty, heartache, pain, weekly doctor appointments, and many of sleepless nights we were still in God's plan. God gives us favor and purpose for our lives. God gave us strength for the journey that we did not realize we possessed. Stop trying to fix your financial woes with your plan and seek God first in all of your endeavors.

Prayer:

Today, Lord, help me to seek Your face and to look to You first for my financial needs. Give me a heart filled with praise for what I see in You; Your trustworthiness, Your peace, Your joy, Your strength, Your grace, Your love. Amen.

Reading:

Matthew 6:33: "But seek first his kingdom and his righteousness, and all these things will be given to you as well."

Application:

List the ways that you are going to make God first in your life today:

DAY 20
Prayer for Spiritual Insight

One of the most uncomfortable times in our marriage was when I transitioned my career from being a corporate accountant and financial analyst to a high school business-education teacher. I have always had a passion for teaching and training teenage kids. I had worked diligently with our youth and young adults in our local and national church for years. The thought of leaving my corporate job to teach full time was frightening. I could not imagine making enough money to sustain our lifestyle as a schoolteacher. In fact, as I did my research on teaching careers, I learned that teachers typically have to work as a student-teacher without pay for a year in order to become a certified teacher in the state of Texas. We knew we could not afford to live off of one income for a year. We needed spiritual insight from God to confirm that I was making the right decision.

In the book of Ephesians, Paul talks about spiritual insight when he says that he had no input into his messages. He meant that God had given him understanding and revelation for his writings and sermons. Ephesians 3:4 says, "In reading this, then you will be able to understand my insight into the mystery of Christ." Paul was given a revelation by God and shares it with the Ephesians so they would have the same insight that was given to him. We prayed every day for God to steer us in the right direction as well as give us the gift of revelation. I specifically needed a teaching job that would be willing to pay me a full-time salary with benefits during my one-year student teaching training. After God confirmed and revealed His will for me to teach, He blessed me with my first teaching job with a school district that agreed to hire me as a paid teacher intern while I finished my alternative-teaching program. I am convinced that I was led to the school district by God.

Even though God had spoken to me and confirmed that I would be teaching business education in the public school system, I had many people to tell me that my chances for getting a job as a business education teacher was slim to none. I was told that a business education teacher job would be hard to find because it's considered a "niche job," a job in "a specialized subject area." In other words, I was not seeking to be a core teacher—that is, English, math, science, history—rather, I was seeking a job as a career and technical education (CTE) teacher that would allow me to specifically teach on business occupational experiences that prepare high school students for careers in the field of business. As disappointing and discouraging as it was to hear such negativity, I kept praying for insight. Oftentimes our minds and spirits are filled with so much negativity from the world that it can distract us from hearing God's voice and leave us feeling confused. I received personal instruction from God, and it was my responsibility to make sure that nothing distracted me from God's will (1 Peter 5:8). As a result of my obedience, I have been blessed financially.

It has truly been a blessing to teach business to such amazing high school students for several years. I learn so much from them. My goal and passion is to teach real-life skills, including financial literacy and business skills to students. My prayer is for each student to leave my class equipped with the financial skills and knowledge needed to survive in the real world, to see Christ in me, and experience the power of His love. Teaching has its challenges, but my passion for what I do gets me through the challenging times. I often repeat in my classroom a quote from Marc Anthony, "If you do what you love, you'll never work a day in your life." I stress the importance for each student to figure out what they are passionate about because *passion* is what will drive them to a successful life.

You may be thinking about leaving your job, changing your career, or making a major life transition during this forty-day financial renewal. This is something that most of us will experience at some point in life. Making a career or job transition calls for spiritual insight. You must seek God for revelation and wait until He gives you a confirmation. Try not to transition prematurely as this could impact your financial plan and future. The mystery was revealed by the spirit to God's holy apostles and prophets in Ephesians 3:5. Your job, ministry, and career goals overlap with your relationships, parenting, and other life goals. Therefore, you have to make sure you are being led by the Holy Spirit. Spiritual insight is so important for you to understand because it allows you to know God's wisdom, God's mind, and God's will for your life. You must have a desire to obey God's Words and have a passion.

Prayer:

Today, Lord, speak to me through Your Word and the words of those who know You. Give me spiritual insight as I go through this financial renewal experience. I am confident that You have begun a good work in my life and will continue until the day of Jesus Christ's return. Amen.

Reading:

Ephesians 3:4: "In reading this, then you will be able to understand my insight into the mystery of Christ."

Application:

What insight has God given you since the start of your forty-day financial renewal experience?

PART III
Renewing My Mind

Do not conform to the pattern of this world, but be transformed by the renewing of your mind. Then you will be able to test and approve what God's will is—his good, pleasing and perfect will.
—Romans 12:2

DAY 21
Receiving God's Blessings

Ken and I have received so many blessing from God. He has sustained us, He has protected us, He has healed us, He has restored us, and He has renewed us. We know that God's blessing helped us to get through our financial struggles. We have always promised God that we would give Him all of the glory, honor, and the praises for His many blessings. This book is meant to bless anyone who is currently or has been in a financial hardship. We truly understand what it means to be in a position of financial need and not be able to get your hands on immediate cash. We learned firsthand that conventional banks do not lend money to people in financial hardships. They typically lend to people who have the wherewithal to pay them back within a certain timeframe and who have good credit scores. Most likely, if you are in a financial hardship, it is going to be reflected in your credit score.

Your credit score comes from your credit report, which is a record of your credit history and financial behavior. Creditors use credit reports to evaluate a consumer's creditworthiness, and decide whether or not to give you credit. Your credit report includes every credit account that you have ever opened. It tells your financial story. It tells how you pay your credit accounts. It reports negative information from different agencies. It also lists overdue taxes, any judgments against you, and any inquiries. When you have poor credit, you will find it difficult to get new credit. You will most likely pay higher interest rates if you are granted credit with poor credit. You should pull your credit report at least once a year from all three of the following major national credit reporting agencies: Equifax, Experian, and TransUnion. Make sure that everything is being report accurately. Review your credit report and start fixing anything that may be affecting your credit score. Be open to working with your creditors. Some creditors are willing to accept a settlement payment up to 50 percent of the debt as payment in full when you explain your financial hardship with them. (see the example Creditor Settlement Letter in the Appendix)

One of the main excuses that we hear in the Body of Christ for why people do not pay tithes is they can't afford to pay because of their obligation to pay outstanding debt or expenses. You must trust that God's blessing over your life will allow all of your needs and wants to be met. God is counting on you to give Him 10 percent of our income and He expects you to be a good steward of the remaining 90 percent. You will receive God's blessings from your obedience of giving Him the 10 percent. He has an amazing way of covering and stretching the 90 percent. The following are the three Bs to receiving God's blessings:

Believe–believe that God will bless you abundantly.
Biblical–biblical stewardship is your covenant with God.
Bless–bless others as God blesses you.

God can bless you beyond your understanding if you trust and obey Him. In Genesis 12:2, it is evident that the Lord is the "great nation" because He is the kingdom in the heavens and on earth. God blessed Abram so that he could bless others. Your true blessing is knowing God and knowing that He will provide all of your needs. His blessings do not leave you in worse financial position. God's blessings mean that you have special favor, mercy, and benefits. Receiving God's blessings moves you to a place of accountability and responsibility.

It is imperative that you understand that the blessing of God should not cause sorrow. According to Proverbs 10:22, "The blessing of the Lord brings wealth, without painful toil for it." If you are looking to rebuild your credit, consider obtaining a secured credit card with a credit limit based on your cash deposit. Once you obtain your secured credit card, charge a few items and pay off the card every month. This will help to increase your credit score. God wants you to be a good steward of His financial resources. He wants to bless you so that you can be a blessing to others.

Prayer:

Today, Lord, I receive Your blessings as divine favor. Your blessings are not just having more money—it's my ability and freedom to enjoy my financial gain. Thank you for blessing me so that I can bless someone else. Amen.

Read:

Genesis 12:2: "I will make you into a great nation, and I will bless you; I will make your name great, and you will be a blessing."

Application:

Who can you bless today? List ways in which you can be a blessing to someone today:

DAY 22
Pay It Forward

The Pay It Forward movement came from a novel and movie called *Pay It Forward*. It is a story about a young boy who did three good deeds for people in need. As a result, everything that the boy wanted was passed on to three other people, and the cycle kept going. This is a giving principle that has been going on since the biblical days. Jesus taught that life is reciprocal, meaning everything that believers give to others will be given back to us. Luke 6:27–38, he says, "But I tell you who hear me: Love your enemies, do good to those who hate you, bless those who curse you, pray for those who mistreat you. If someone strikes you on one cheek, turn to him the other also. If someone takes your cloak, do not stop him from taking your tunic. Give to everyone who asks you, and if anyone takes what belongs to you, do not demand it back. Do to others as you would have them do to you."

We are sure you are probably thinking: Why is paying it forward important? What does paying it forward have to do with a financial renewal? This is about renewing your mind about your money, giving, spending, and about how you treat others. "Paying it forward" is doing something kind for someone. Kindness is the quality of being friendly, generous, and considerate. There is a saying that "kindness doesn't cost a thing". The act of kindness is contagious and spreads quickly as you show kindness toward others. Simply smiling at someone is a powerful act of kindness that blesses others. We enjoy demonstrating this in the classroom and workshops. We greet our audience with a big authentic smile for a few seconds before we began speaking. Most of the time the entire audience will respond to us and each other with a smile. They tend to mimic our smile because we have triggered the same emotional state in them. According to Galatians 5:22, kindness is a principle from one of the fruits of the Spirit.

Kindness is the same principle as pay it forward. To pay it forward is to respond to a person's kindness by being kind to someone else. It's when you do a good deed for others without expecting anything in return. Instead, the recipient is to pay it forward to someone else in need. We are reminded of a situation after Kennedi's death in May 2005 when we received an unexpected personal check from our bishop and his wife who were serving in the Dallas Fort Worth region. We were so appreciative of their love and support. We, in turn, used some of the money to bless other children who were sick like Kennedi. In spite of our financial struggles, we kept giving. All of our giving was exhilarating.

More and more people got involved in giving to our family. We received stacks of cards with checks every week. We did not know half of the people who were sending us checks. As we received, we continued to give to others in need. After that powerful experience of paying it forward, we continue to do it today. Occasionally I will pay for someone's coffee at Starbucks and watch how people respond to paying it forward. Buying someone a cup of coffee might not seem like much, but if everyone did something good for someone else, then the cycle of giving and kindness can make not only your organization a better place, but also this world a better place. It always amazes me how the cycle automatically keeps going when you pay it forward. Once you do a good deed for someone, that person is usually eager to do good for someone else. Every time I do this type of kind act, I feel blessed. We want you to experience the power of paying it forward.

Be on alert on how you can pay it forward today. It could be giving a smile, a service, money, or a gift to someone that you do not know. This could be someone in your community, on your job, in your church. When that person thanks you and/or asks how they can repay you, tell them that you would like for them to pay it forward. As someone does something nice for you, start thinking about three people that you can do something nice to as well. You will receive everything that you give to others. As God blesses you with monetary blessing, it gives you an opportunity to share monetary blessing and the gospel of Jesus Christ with others. It is an amazing experience!

Prayer:

Today, Lord, I will be a blessing to someone because you have blessed me. I will respond to your blessings by doing good deeds for one to three people without asking for anything in return. Amen.

Read:

Luke 6:35–36: "But love your enemies, do good to them, and lend to them without expecting to get anything back. Then your reward will be great, and you will be children of the

Most High, because he is kind to the ungrateful and wicked. Be merciful, just as your Father is merciful."

Application:

Do three random acts of kindness to family, friend, or a stranger. Describe how it made you feel to do something kind for others:

DAY 23
Reaping and Sowing

Every summer we look forward to going to Fort Valley, Georgia to visit family. One of our favorite places to visit is the Lane Southern Orchards located just outside of Fort Valley, in the heart of Middle Georgia. This place is famous for growing peaches, pecans, and strawberries. We love picking our very own juicy strawberries. One day while we were picking strawberries, we met one of the farmers. He shared some interesting and intriguing facts about how the strawberries are planted, grown, and harvested. We were so fascinated how one single seed that sprouts can yield so many rows of strawberries.

We learned that the farmers start planting the strawberry seeds in rows in early October and they start blooming around March, followed by ripening from early April through June. Through the process of sowing the seeds, we reap the benefit of picking and eating the delicious strawberries during the summer. As Christian, we live a life of reaping and sowing. The first seeds were sown in our hearts by Jesus when He died for our sins. His seed grows like a tree as we saturate our lives with the Word of God.

In Galatians 6:7, Paul refers to reaping what we sow in the Bible when he says, "Let us not become weary in doing good, for at the proper time we will reap a harvest if we do not give up." The Galatians had allowed their love for Christ to diminish. They had become weary. They were being attacked by different forces, which made them become weary and frustrated. There are two sorts of sowing, one to the flesh and the other to the Spirit. Those who live a carnal life must expect "fruit" that produces misery. On the other hand, those who live a life under the guidance and influences of the Holy Spirit must expect "fruit" that reaps a life of abundant blessings. Ken and I often give out of our need. The more we need, the more we give. The more we give, the more we expect from God. Everything that we give, God has a miraculous way of multiplying it.

There have been several occasions when God has told us to give someone or an organization a lump sum of money from our savings account. I remember a time when Ken wrote a check to a church for $2,500 because he said God told him to do it. At the time, we needed to get about $3,500 worth of car repairs. I gave him that look like, *I hope you are right about this.* He gave me a look of assurance that made me feel comfortable. About two weeks later, Ken called me at work to let me know that we had received two checks in the mail that were larger than we had given to the church. I shouted so loud that my coworkers ran to my desk to make sure I was okay. I told them that I was shouting for joy because I had just received some great news. Not only were we able to get our car fixed, but we were able to get some much-needed things done around our home. That is one of many examples of us reaping what we had sown.

We realize that there will be times when you may become weary because of different attacks or financial setback. It is a natural instinct to make sense of the things that happen in your life. You may find yourself spending a lot of time trying to figure out why certain things happened to you. If you are like us, you want to know what it means and how to fix it. When it does not make sense, your human instinct is to start rationalizing it in your mind and filling in blanks based on your perception and perspectives. It is important for you to start paying close attention to the stories that you concoct in your mind about yourself and your finances. You will find that most of the things are not true. The devil uses lies and deceit to trap you into negative thinking. John 8:44 says, "You belong to your father, the devil, and you want to carry out your father's desires. He was a murderer from the beginning, not holding to the truth, for there is no truth in him. When he lies, he speaks his native language, for he is a liar and the father of lies." Don't believe the devil's lies! Keep sowing seeds of kindness, love, positivity, and financial blessings even in the midst of your weariness.

You may feel that giving to others will take away from your budget, but we challenge you to trust God. Some days it may seem like your "seeds" are not producing an immediate crop, that you are not "reaping" God's blessing, but continue to sow your seeds and believe there will be a harvest. There is no timetable for the harvest of life. Your season will come. When you "walk by faith, not by sight" (2 Corinthians 5:7) it requires you to go to a place that you do not know or understand. Trust God and He will reveal His plan as you walk in your obedience to Him.

Prayer:

Today, Lord, as I sow my finances, I expect a harvest of my finances. As I sow love, I expect a harvest of love. As I give willingly for Your name's sake, I expect to receive a hundred-fold return. Amen.

Reading:

Galatians 6:7:" Do not be deceived: God cannot be mocked. A man reaps what he sows."

Application:

How can God count on you today to be a sower who is willing to sow?

DAY 24
Living in Financial Peace

Everyone desires to live in financial peace. We believe that is what God desires for all of His children. When we had finally worked ourselves out of our financial hardship, it felt so exhilarating not having to worry about the stress of the enormous amount of debt. It felt great to get paid, to pay our tithes, put money in our savings, pay all of our bills on time, and still have money left over. That is when we decided to start living. It has been over ten years now since we added yearly vacations to our budget. We feel that this is a great opportunity to spend quality time with our family. It is our time to get away from the daily demands of life and ministry to enrich our marriage. It allows our children to witness us having fun, laughter, and enjoying life without worrying about financial matters.

Pastors, ministers, and church leaders, please take care of your souls! In Ken's early-morning meditation reflecting on God's rest, peace, restoration and power, he often prays for pastors and leaders. Many leaders experience spiritual burnout and are feeling physically exhausted. He says, "The thirty-six years that I have been in pastoral leadership and ministry has been an overwhelming blessing, but not without enormous challenges and sacrifice." Ken suggests that every pastor, minister, and church leader should:

1. Take a day off for yourself.
2. Remember you can't do God's ministry without God.
3. Stay in touch with God so you can effectively minister to God's people.
4. Build meaningful friendships. Friendships are essential because isolation will render you extremely lonely.
5. Find balance between ministry and family life (your family needs you more than we are available at times).
6. Take some time to minister to yourself!

If your weeks are anything like Ken's—i.e., sixty to seventy-five hours every week, sermon prep ten to twelve hours and preaching, Bible study prep four to six hours before teaching, community outreach fifteen to twenty hours, meetings, revivals, vision casting, event planning, office hours for availability to the Body of Christ, personal prayer time two hours daily, sick calls, death calls, weddings, funerals and after care, counseling, late-night tragedy calls, early morning hospital visits, staff meetings, returning phone calls, traveling for ministry, social justice ministry, etc. you need to allow yourself some downtime for rest and restoration. If you don't come apart from ministry for rest, prayer, and relaxation, ministry will tear you apart. We are praying for you today. God loves you and knows exactly what you need, *peace*!

It is so peaceful and enjoyable when we take time out of our hectic schedules for recreation. Recreation is what we do for rest, relaxation, and enjoyment. It is our time to "re-create," to take time to renew and restore our mind, body, and spirit. We typically start planning for our family vacations about a year in advance because this is when we are able to get the best deals and rates. Our goal is to visit a new place each year. We discuss what each family member enjoys doing as a group, then we narrow it down to our top choices. Once we decide where we want to go and confirm the dates, we create a separate budget called "vacation budget". This money is typically put aside in a different bank account.

Since I am a schoolteacher, summer is typically a great time for our family vacations. We make a list of all of our projected vacation expenses, i.e., airplane tickets, hotel, food, activities, etc. and we both start putting a small portion toward our vacation budget for a year. By the time we are ready to go on vacation, we are worry free and excited about building wonderful memories with our family. We look forward to coming back refreshed, energized, and ready to refocus. We have talked to many church leaders who do not take the time to go on vacation. We always encourage them to make time for rest and relaxation so they too can feel a sense of restoration and peace. There are so many health benefits of taking a vacation. It reduces stress, it is good for your heart, it is great for your mental health, and great for your relationships.

Even if you cannot go on your "dream vacation," take time for a "staycation" - a vacation spent close to home or spent at home enjoying local attractions. In 2 Thessalonians 3:16, Paul addressed the church in his letter as he expounded on peace. The kind of peace that Paul was referring to was the peace that believers only find in Jesus Christ. This characteristic of God would be most meaningful to reflect upon in light of the intense spiritual battle that raged all around the Thessalonians. The peace that God gives us takes up residence in our hearts and brings the peace that surpasses all understanding (Philippians 4:7).

In this world, the only true peace is the peace that we find in God. I am reminded of time that I taught financial literacy at our church denomination national church conference. After teaching, a young lady walked up to me after my workshop and asked, "What does it mean to live in financial peace?" I immediately responded from my perspective, "Financial peace is when all of your bills are current and you do not have to continuously worry about your ability to meet all of your financial obligations." She looked at me with a look of frustration and replied, "That is my goal in life." I was happy to pray with her and give her some tips to help her get on the right track with her finances.

Without great trials, you cannot experience victory. If you notice, the Lord reveals Himself in all of your trials. As you walk with the Lord, He will give you the peace and joy that you so deserve. Make time for rest and relaxation so that you too can feel a sense of restoration and peace. Start planning your vacation today.

Prayer:

Today, Lord, I desire to live in financial peace. Help me to take time to renew and restore my mind, body, and spirit so I can find balance in my life. When I worry, and become anxious about my finances, help me to avoid the easy way out. Give me the courage and strength to have peace in You and your promises. Amen.

Reading:

2 Thessalonians 3:16: "Now may the Lord of peace himself give you peace at all times and in every way. The Lord be with all of you."

Application:

Is there a conflict/s in your life and finances that is compromising genuine peace? List them and pray for peace.

DAY 25
The Great I Am

Many people find it difficult to stick to a budget. It truly takes a lot of discipline. Are you one of those who constantly get off track with your budget? Think about why you cannot seem to stick to your budget. Think about why you spend and what you are spending your money on. Do you tend to buy things that you will never use? Do you spend more time shopping than hanging out with your family and friends? Are all of your credit cards over the limit? If any of these habits sound like you, you may be considered a compulsive spender. I know all too well what it means to shop out of depression. I found myself using shopping as a medicine to numb myself and to take my mind off my problems. As you know, it is only a temporary fix. After I purchased it, I would feel even worse especially after Ken spent several minutes fusing at me for getting off our budget.

It is very common for compulsive spenders to shop out of boredom, to relieve stress, depression, and out of loneliness. I have to pray for strength regularly not to be a compulsive spender. I realize that faith without works is dead (James 2:14). I know that I have to put in the work to make responsible choices. In fact, that is one of the main reasons I do not carry cash. If I carry cash, I will pinch off of it until it is gone. We put our debit and credit cards on a daily maximum limit with automatic alerts when we are getting close to our spending limit. This helps us to stay within our budget and keeps us from overspending. We pray that God can give you strength to stop some of your destructive behaviors during this financial renewal process. The enemy will use compulsive spending to keep you in financial bondage.

In Exodus 3:14, God told Moses to go to Pharaoh and bring the Israelites out of Egypt. Moses asked God, "Who am I? Who shall I say sent me?" God said to tell them "I am who I am sent you." God had already revealed Himself and demonstrated His promises to Moses in a bush. Moses could not confront Pharoah within his own strength. He needed God for the task at hand. "I AM" as God's name speaks of His eternal self-existence, the existence of everyone, and everything else is contingent upon Him. Our knowledge of God is dependent on the extent to which He reveals Himself to us. You may be struggling with sticking with your budget. God is faithful even when we are inconsistent with Him. In 2 Timothy 2:13, it says, "If we are faithless, he remains faithful, for he cannot disown himself." If you have gotten off track with your budget, do not beat yourself up. A habit is a routine of behavior that is repeated regularly. Whether good or bad, your life is a sum of all of your habits. It is time to get in a habit of budgeting your money.

We will not try to give you some special number for the amount of days it takes to formulate a new spending and budgeting habit, but we will tell you that anything that you do repeatedly will eventually become a new habit. You will find yourself doing it without even thinking about it. One of our favorite quotes is by Zig Ziglar, "Your input determines your outlook. Your outlook determines your output, and your output determines your future." When we first started budgeting our money, it was difficult because we were in the habit of buying whatever we felt like buying without thinking about other bills that were due. But, having our weekly budgeting meetings helps us to be accountable and more responsible with our money.

We pray before and after we discuss our budget. After a while, sticking to our budget became a habit. Now we stick to it without putting much thought in to it. What are you willing to input so that you can stick to your budget? You can start with keeping track of your daily and weekly purchases by writing down everything that you spend. This will help you to stick with your budget. Trust the "Great I Am" who can give you the strength to stick to your budget. You can do it!

Prayer:

Today, Lord, I acknowledge that I have been inconsistent with my finances, but Lord you always remain the same. You are never inconsistent; I know I can always count on You, even when You can't count on me. Help me to be a responsible, disciplined steward who sticks to my budget. Amen.

Reading:

Exodus 3:14: "God said to Moses, "I am who I am. This is what you are to say to the Israelites: 'I am has sent me to you."

Application:

How can you be more consistent with your finances?

DAY 26
Leaving a Legacy

Have you ever thought about what type of legacy you will leave? Will it be lasting? Will you leave behind a home, money, and/or other personal possessions? No matter how you live your life or what you leave behind, you will leave behind some kind of legacy. You can't escape it! Your legacy will impact those who know you, either for the good or the bad. You must choose how you will behave, and what kind of legacy you will leave. Most people want to be remembered, to be significant, to feel that they have contributed something to the world. For some of us, this is what drives us to keep doing ministry, help others, and give to others. For others, it may not cross their minds until they experience a near death experience.

Every time Ken and I lose a friend, family, and/or church member to death, we immediately connect death to our own legacy. We often wonder: "What will people say about me?" "What legacy will I leave here on earth?" Most people do not like to think or talk about dying. It is viewed as morbid thoughts and is uncomfortable to discuss in most families. However, planning now for your family's future not only helps to protect you from financial hardship, but it can also keep your family financially secure when you transition to be with Lord. There have been many situations where Ken had to serve as both the pastor and mediator after a church member loses a loved one to death because the deceased did not have a will in place.

We have witnessed family feuds over things such as furniture and family photo albums. A lot of confusion can be avoided by simply having a will in place. Whenever a person dies without a will, it is called dying intestate. If it goes to probate court, it can take a long time for the decease's assets to be divided and distributed by the government. You do not necessarily need an attorney to write your will. As long as you comply with the laws of your state, you can write your own will that can stand up in a court of law. You can either draft it on a computer, hand write it, or create one through an online program.

If you decide to do it yourself, you can either use a template from a free legal documents online source or you can write it. It should clearly be labeled as "Last Will and Testament." Be sure to state your full name, address, social security number, and birth date. List the names of the people who will receive your assets (i.e., personal property, real estate, money, jewelry, clothes, photos, furniture, etc.). Make sure you clearly outline how the property will be transferred to beneficiaries. List the full name of the executor, the person who will manage all of your business affairs such as your will, funeral expenses, burial, and other bills. If you have minor children, you need to name a guardian who will be responsible for caring for your children and managing an estate on their behalf. Lastly, be sure to sign and date your will and write that it revokes any previously made will or codicil. If you have a large estate with tax issues or if it is too complicated, contact a probate attorney to draw up and manage your will.

We have seen it time and time again when a loved one dies and no one in the family has enough money to cover the funeral and burial expenses. Our family experienced this in 2005 when we realized we did not have insurance on our daughter, Kennedi, at the time of her death. We often wonder how our lives would have been different if we would have purchased life insurance for Kennedi. We definitely learned some valuable lessons from that experience. We make sure that everyone in our house is covered with insurance. If you are wondering whether you should purchase life insurance or not, ask yourself the following questions: If I died today, how would my family be impacted financially? Could my family afford the home that I currently live in? Will my family have enough money to manage our household expenses? If you have answered no to these questions, you need life insurance protection so that you can leave your family with the financial resources that will keep the family out of financial risk. You can also leave a financial legacy that can be passed down generations.

If you do not have a life insurance, consider getting one during this forty-day financial renewal experience. Choosing the right life insurance can provide you and your family with financial security. The more financial responsibilities you have, the more coverage you need, particularly if you have others who depend on your income for support. As the insured, the face value of your life-insurance policy will be paid to your beneficiary when you transition to be with the Lord. Whoever you list as your beneficiary will receive all of your benefits from your policy. Make sure you make changes to your beneficiary when your marital status changes.

There are three main types of life insurance: term, whole life, and endowment. Term life insurance protects you only for a specific period of time. Whole life insurance is a basic lifetime insurance that protects you as long as you pay your premiums. Endowment insurance pays the face value of the policy to your beneficiaries if you pass before the endowment period ends. Everyone has different needs as it relates to life insurance coverage. It takes careful planning to choose the one best for you and your family. Consult with an insurance agent on which type of coverage you should choose and the amount of protection you need.

Once you select the right life insurance plan, add your insurance payments to your monthly budget under your list of monthly expenses. God appreciates when you make wise decisions. In the story of Joseph, his wise planning saved the nation of Egypt and the people of Israel (Genesis 41). Having life insurance can guarantee income for your survivors. Use it as a way to protect your assets and to leave a legacy for your heirs.

Prayer:

Today, Lord, thank you for positioning me to leave a legacy for my children and the next generation. Give me the knowledge to put a financial plan in place that will safeguard my family when I leave this earth to be with You. Amen.

Reading:

Psalm 78:4: "We will not hide them from their children, but tell to the coming generation the glorious deeds of the Lord, and his might, and the wonders that he has done."

Application:

What legacy will you leave for future generations in your family? Do you have life insurance? If so, make sure all of your information is correct. If not, call a local agent today for more information on purchasing a plan.

DAY 27
Jesus Promised He'll Take Care of Me

Our choir sings a song by the Chicago Mass Choir called "Jesus Promised." This is one of the songs that our choir sings regularly that tends to make the entire church smile. They lyrics go, "O how wonderful it is, Jesus promised he'll take care of me. I can call him in the morning. I can call him in the middle of the night. And when I call him, he'll make everything alright. It does not matter how big the problem may be. Jesus promised he'll take care of me." Every time the choir sings this song, I purposely look around the church at all of the faces. By the looks on their faces, I always sense that everyone has a personal testimony about how Jesus has taken care of them in their most trying times in life. The word "promise" is a person's assurance that they will or will not do something. God has made us many promises throughout the Bible. One of His many promises is that He will supply all of our needs (Philippians 4:19). God does not lie. He does not change His mind. He does not break promises. Unlike God, humankind in our imperfections is capable of breaking promises, but you can always trust that God's promises will come to pass.

Metaphorically speaking, when you are in a life storm, you should never make any major life decisions because your vision and thoughts can be distorted by the debris of the storm.

Most of the time a crisis or tragedy naturally causes stress, confusion, anxiety, and desperation, which is why it is so important to calm down and wait on God for direction. In Luke 3:14, John's ministry was to bring the people from their sins so he gave them many warnings and exhortations. He tells the soldiers that they should be cautioned against the temptations of their employments. He conveys to them that no one can accept Christ's salvation without true repentance. I know too well the danger of making a major life decision during a time of grief.

In 2003, a few months after I had birthed Kennedi, against Ken's better judgment, I went searching for a car without him. I had been having major car trouble and was growing more desperate and impatient each day to get rid of the old car so we could purchase a new car. One day I checked our mail and there was an advertisement that seemed to be the answer to my car problems. There was a letter with a single car key addressed directly to me that read, "Bring this key to our car lot and drive away with your car today." Yes! I took the bait. I threw on my clothes and drove to Denton, Texas with hopes to drive back with my new car. As soon as I drove up, I had several salesmen to approach me about buying a car.

However, there was one particular fast-talking, aggressive, deliberate salesman who refused to accept no for an answer. He instantaneously targeted me and made me his customer. I handed him my letter and asked him about the "key to my new car." He told me it was simply an advertisement to lure people to the car lot. I thought to myself, *I am one of many suckers who had fallen for this.* He pressured me to find a car to test-drive. After I test-drove the car of my choice, all kinds of shenanigans began. He had me in his office filling out a credit application and had pulled by credit report before I finished the application. The next thing I knew, he was trading in my old car and asking me for an enormous down payment for the new car. I told him that I did not have that amount of money. He said, "That is fine, just write me a personal check for the total amount of the down payment and I will hold it here in my office. All you have to do is make monthly payments on the check. After you have made all of the monthly cash payments to cover the check, I will hand you back your check."

He assured me that it was perfectly fine and that he did these types of arrangements with most of his customers. I was very uneasy with the deal, but under pressure, I agreed with it. When I got back home with the car and explained the agreement to Ken, he was livid. He was upset with me for accepting the deal, and he was upset with the salesman for taken advantage of me. Ken immediately demanded that we go back to the car lot to get my old car back and the personal check that I had left with the salesman. When we arrived at the car lot, the salesman seemed to give us the runaround and avoided us. This went on for several weeks. We learned that he had deposited my check and sent over the paperwork to finalize the deal the same week of our agreement. I was stuck with the new car and a personal check that I did not have the funds to cover. Eventually, I had to report his fraudulent and deceptive behavior to the senior managers of the car dealer, the corporate office, and to our bank, which caused him to face some major consequences.

I will never forget the last conversation that the salesman and I had after I had reported him. In a very vindictive tone, he told me that he would make sure that I paid for what I had done to him for the rest of my life. I did not understand his threat until years later. He purposely filed a lawsuit against me in the criminal court for "theft by check" for the check that he had tricked me into writing. Then he reported me to the police, and a warrant was issued for my arrest. It should have been filed in the civil court, but he knew it would be filed as a felony in the criminal court because of the amount.

I should have hired an attorney immediately, but I did not understand the magnitude of the charges until later. Without an attorney, I went to the sheriff's office to explain that I had been scammed, but they were not interested in my story and proceeded to make their arrest based on the active warrant. I was there for a couple of hours, long enough for them to go through processing, but it felt like eternity. To make a long, long nightmare short, I went to court for the charges and was found not guilty. The car lot had to pay for my legal expenses. The case has been expunged, however, the negative stigma of the charges has affected my life for over thirteen years. It never seems to go away because new agencies keep buying and selling old arrest records.

I have been laughed at, mocked, ridiculed, and even missed out on job opportunities because of the charges. For every missed opportunity, God blessed me with a great opportunity because He promised to take care of me. Unfortunately, most people are not privy to the end results—that I was found not guilty of the charges and it was expunged. They typically are so alarmed and shocked about the charges that they take the limited information, run with it, and make judgment without knowing all of the facts. We share this experience with you as a testimony and life lesson.

When we do things our way instead of God's way, expect the consequences that go along with it. In spite of the damaging documents and data that continue to plague my name, Jesus has taken care of me. You too may be dealing with an embarrassing situation. Do not walk around in shame or fear.

Be thankful for the life lessons that you have learned from your experience and the strength that you gained from it.

Use your experience to help someone else with your story because your story gives His-story the glory! I am sure that you can relate to someone deceiving you, lying on you, and/or defaming your name and not being able to do anything about it. The Bible says, "No weapon formed against you shall prosper, and every tongue which rises against you in judgment You shall condemn. This is the heritage of the servants of the Lord, And their righteousness is from Me, Says the Lord." (Isaiah 54:17)

Try not to make any major life decisions during a time of grief or during a major trial. You may experience feelings of regret if you make long-term financial decisions based on a short-term situation. You can find hope and assurance in the fact that God will take care of you. If you are faced with dishonest or fraudulent business practices, do not attempt to handle it on our own. It is to your advantage to contact an attorney or consumer advocates to help you. There are numerous government and nongovernment agencies that can protect you as a consumer. We have listed several as a resource in the appendix. Trust God's Word and His promises that Jesus will always take care of you. Now that deserves a praise break! Praise Him even when you do not see how He will take care of your situation.

Prayer:

Today, Lord, I am standing on Your promises because You are my all in all. Help me to not make any major life decisions based on a temporary financial situation. Give me strength to wait on You during hard times. Thank you for protecting me, taking care of me and fulfilling all Your promises. Amen.

Reading:

Luke 3:14: "Soldiers also asked him, "And we, what shall we do?" And he said to them, "Do not extort money from anyone by threats or by false accusation, and be content with your wages."

Application:

List at list three attorneys or organizations that can help you if you are ever faced with fraudulent business practices.

DAY 28
My Latter Will Be Greater

Do you remember a time in your life when you were not concerned about your finances? You might be thinking the only time you can remember not being concerned about finances is when you were a kid still living at home. At least you knew it was not your problem when there was not enough money to cover all of the household bills. If your family was like ours, they did whatever they needed to do to provide in those days. Being raised in the church, we always understood that God provides for His people. Ken and I often talk about how our mothers and grandmothers always found a way to make ends meet.

I am still amazed how my eighty-four-year-old grandmother was able to pay off her house with her modest income that came from what she refers to as "day work." This was another name for a housekeeper or maid. Grandma worked for a different family every day for five to six days a week to help my grandfather care for their seven children and to pay for their living expenses until he transitioned. After thirty years of marriage, my grandmother was forced to rebuild her life without my grandfather. With resilience and perseverance, she was left to take care of their seven children and all her personal finances. Now that we are adults raising our own family, we are appreciative of how they were able to take care of their families singlehandedly without the same resources that we are privy to.

Our grandmothers could not imagine making the kinds of salaries that we make in our generation, yet they seem to be successful managing their finances with much less. God is doing more for us than He did for our parents, grandparents, and great grandparents because He is a God of increase. We learned how to survive hardship from previous generations. Anytime you experience a loss, i.e., death of a loved one, job loss, separation or divorce, you must accept a new normalcy. Ken and I define "new normalcy" as accepting and adjusting to a new way of life while embracing a new situation. New normalcy forces us to rebuild our lives. Ken and I have had to go through the process of rebuilding several times as we were faced with different financial challenges. Rebuilding is what the people in the book of Haggai experienced (Haggai 1–2).

The Lord promised the people that the temple would be filled with His glory and that peace would be provided in the temple. Haggai 2:9 says, "The glory of this present house will be greater than the glory of the former house,' says the Lord Almighty. 'And in this place I will grant peace,' declares the Lord Almighty." The temple had been destroyed, and they had been instructed to rebuild the temple. After fifteen years, the temple still was not completed because they were more concerned with building their own houses than the house of the Lord. The scripture demonstrates how the glory of the latter day will be greater than the glory of the former day. God wants you to know that your financial position will be even greater, not because of what you are doing, but because of what God is doing with you and your finances. You might be in a place of rebuilding during this forty-day financial renewal.

Rebuilding is a process. You must allow yourself to grieve. Everyone grieves differently, so do not allow people to define your grief process. God brings us to a place of peace and comfort in our loss.

Write a daily journal to help cope with your pain associated with your loss. Set your priorities, create your financial plan that includes your new income and expenses, and build a strong support system. It takes dedication and hard work to rebuild. There will be challenges and obstacles that will come up, but you can build a new life that will be greater than your latter. Always remember that God has a plan for you greater than anything you can imagine.

Prayer:

Today, Lord, I thank you for blessing my ancestors who paved the way for me. Just as the Jews built Your spiritual Temple, I must also build a spiritual temple filled with Your glory and peace. I know You are making my latter greater than my former! Amen.

Reading:

Haggai 2:9. "The glory of this present house will be greater than the glory of the former house,' says the Lord Almighty. 'And in this place I will grant peace,' declares the Lord Almighty."

Application:

What are some ways that you can rebuild your personal finances?

DAY 29
Give Us Our Daily Bread

One way that God allows his children to stay connected with Him is through prayer. Through your prayers you are able to communicate with God, make your request known to God, confess your sins to God, give adoration to God, praises to God, and to give thanks to God. Many believers learned how to pray as a child. One of the first prayers that we learned was the Lord's Prayer. The Lord's Prayer was recorded in Matthew 6:9–13 and Luke 11:2–4. It is the prayer that Jesus used to instruct His disciples how to pray. Some people recite it in unison in church, some sing it at weddings and other sacred occasions, some recite it in their daily prayer, and some meditate on each portion in their private time with God. The Lord's Prayer is our request to God to supply both our physical and material needs.

There have been times in our marriage when we wondered how we were going to make it through the week financially. There was not a person who we could call about our situation who was trustworthy and confidential. We have discovered that it is very difficult to work through personal trials when your life is on public display. Therefore, it is important for leaders to find a safe and sacred place to land. Every leader should have at least one friend that they can confide in. Due to the lack of trust, many church leaders are suffering in silence, which forces them to internalize their emotions. I once visited a therapist who described this type of behavior as a rubber band being stretched until it reaches its breaking point. We believe that is why many pastors have reached their breaking point, i.e., melt down, burnout, quitting, health-related issues, or death. We pray that you will seek God for a spiritual brother or sister in Christ who can be a safe and sacred place to land. If you are suffering in silence, we encourage you to see a therapist.

We remember days when we would just pray the Lord's Prayer during our time of financial despair. One thing we both can attest to, God always provides all of our needs. We have never missed a meal, and we very seldom missed church. This was a time to draw nearer to God. He is our bread of life that satisfies our spiritual hunger. When we ask God for our daily bread, we are acknowledging Him as Jehovah-Jireh, our Provider. (Gen. 22:14) God will provide all of your needs. He smiles when He sees you trusting Him to provide all of your financial needs. Proverbs 30:8 says, "Keep falsehood and lies far from me; give me neither poverty nor riches, but give me only my daily bread." Solomon prayed that God would simply give him "the food that is needed" for life, which is repeated in Jesus's prayer in Matthew 6:11 when he taught us how to pray. He said, "Give us this day our daily bread." In other words, believers are to ask God for what we need. This is a brief prayer that reiterates the importance of having a God-centered perspective of life.

God expects the Body of Christ to remain content, humble, and truthful, free from any temptation to deny God's name. We have witnessed many Christians who treat God like a magician or a "genie in a bottle". They think they can snap their fingers and magically get what they want from God. They will pray to God only when they want something from Him or when they are facing some major life crisis. When life is seemingly going well, they will say that they are too busy to come to church or to do ministry. But as soon as they lose a job, get sick, get into a major financial bind, or other crisis, they run back to church and are the first to run to the altar for prayer. We are definitely not saying that you should not pray when you are going through a crisis; we are saying you should be praying every day. God wants us to trust that He will give us our daily bread.

Prayer:

Today, Lord, give me my daily bread, keep lack far from me, and don't put more on me than I can bear. Thank you for keeping me each day and for the many blessings that you have bestowed upon my life. Amen.

Read:

Proverbs 30:8: "Keep falsehood and lies far from me; give me neither poverty nor riches, but give me only my daily bread."

Application:

Reflect on what it means to you to pray for your daily bread.

DAY 30
Growing in Love

Love is so powerful! Ken and I are convinced that Kennedi was placed in our lives to help us grow in love. We often think about how much we loved Kennedi during her short time with us on earth. We were so blinded by our love for her that we would often forget about all of our financial problems. It did not matter anymore. We would even forget about all of her disabilities. Her severe brain injury caused her to be disabled and solely depend on us to care for her. It seemed like God had miraculously increased some of Kennedi's senses due to her multiple disabilities. She was unable to talk, but somehow, she figured out how to communicate with us through her eyes. It was so fascinating to see her show expressions through those beautiful brown eyes.

We knew when she was happy, when she was sad, when she was in pain, when she wanted us to hold or hug her. We even felt her deep love for us through her eyes. She had an angelic presence that would make us so uncomfortable when she gave us that piercing stare. Some days we could feel Jesus looking at us through our baby girl. This was confirmed one day when we visited her neurologist. She was about twelve months. We asked her neurologist if she would ever walk or talk, and he said with a very intrigued look on his face, "Mr.

and Mrs. Hollingshed, based on the severity of her brain injury, she should not have made it out of the NICCU. I cannot explain medically why she is alive and how she is able to do the things that she is doing. It must be your love and the love of God that is keeping Kennedi here, so cherish each day with her." We knew it was God's power of love sustaining her. Kennedi viewed us as her protector, but her presence always made us feel like she was protecting us.

His response led me to my next question, "How long will she live?" He replied, "Based on the severity of her brain injury, she can live up to about five years old. Every patient is different." He assured us that we would see a decline in Kennedi's health the older she got. It was a tough pill to swallow, but we tried to accept his timeline. We felt like we had at least four more years to spend with Kennedi, and therefore we wanted to live each day as if it were going to be her last. We also asked the doctor if she was strong enough for us to take her to Disney World in Orlando, Florida. He responded with great enthusiasm, "Absolutely, continue to love her!" However, we sensed that he knew more, but he wanted us to focus on loving her and spending quality time with her each day. Kennedi passed about one year later after that visit.

The love in our home was so intense that it made our love for each other even more intense. Still today, Ken and I have an unbreakable bond. I am sure the kind of love that we experienced with Kennedi is similar to the kind of love that motivated God to send His Son to the cross. John 3:16 tells us, "For God so *loved* the world, that he gave his only begotten Son, that whosoever believeth in him should not perish, but have everlasting life". When Jesus is at the center of your heart, not only will you grow in love, but everything and anyone in your life will be impacted by your love. In John 14:23, "Jesus replied, anyone who loves me will obey my teaching. My Father will love them, and we will come to them and make our home with them." Do not get so consumed with your financial matters and other personal matters that you forget to express your love to those who matter most, your family and friends. Ask God to help you to grow in love each day of your life.

Prayer:

Today, Lord, may I love You in all things and above all things. Help me to reach the joy that You have prepared for me in Heaven. All that is good comes from Your love for me. Help me to grow in love daily. Amen.

Reading:

John 14:23: "Jesus replied, anyone who loves me will obey my teaching. My Father will love them, and we will come to them and make our home with them."

Application:

Express your love for a least three people today by making a call, sending a text, a card, or a love note. List their names.

PART IV
Renewing My Financial Plan

And my God will meet all your needs according to the riches of his glory in Christ Jesus.
—Philippians 4:19

DAY 31
Facing Fears

There is a popular acronym for the word *fear* in the Body of Christ that Ken and I refer to often: FEAR–false evidence appearing real. Fear is a realistic emotion. Fear is defined as a response to physical and emotional danger. It is natural for us to protect ourselves from any type of danger. Our bad experiences can trigger our fears. Even in the midst of our fears, God is doing something great. When Ken and I were in financial trouble, we constantly lived in fear. At one time, our fears had completely controlled our lives. It was almost debilitating. Somehow we had replaced God being at the center of our lives with our fears. As a result, everything surrounding our lives was driven by our fears. After the trauma of Kennedi's death, we were scared to allow our youngest son, Kingston, to sleep in his own bed even though he was perfectly healthy. I remember both of us suddenly waking up in the middle of the night to check his pulse or heartbeat.

Kingston slept between us until he got big enough to kick and head-butt us in the middle of the night as he tossed and turned. That is when we knew it was time to transition him to his own bed and to get over our fear of him dying in the middle of the night. We were even scared to face all of the debt. We were scared to face our credit report. We were scared that the cars would get repossessed or that we would get evicted from our home. We were scared that our church family would get tired of all our issues and put us out of the church. We were scared that I would get fired from my corporate job. We were scared that we would lose it all and not be able to care for our children. We were afraid that one of us would get tired and file for divorce or get sick. We were scared that everyone was going to find out how bad things really were for us. The list of fears went on and on. We were just a bundle of walking nerves. This kind of fear was far worse than the best horror movie that we had ever seen.

Anytime there is a threat in our lives, it pushes us to go into flight or fight mode. We chose to fight. We knew our fear was caused by the enemy, not by God, and thus we needed to know how to defeat the enemy. Ken explained to me that when he trained in the army, there was a process to prepare him and the other soldiers for war. He shared how the military prepared them mentally and physically for the task at hand. He also shared that the Lord told him that we were going to have to become Christian soldiers and prepare for spiritual battle. The Bible specifically speaks of spiritual battles and gives us great tools on how to fight our battles. It tells us to "put on the whole armor of God," according to Ephesians 6:10–20. Facing our fears was the turning point for us to face our fears of financial troubles.

Renewing our finances required us to acknowledge our fears and find the courage to take them on. You cannot fix anything that you are unable to face. We wrote down every single fear and wrote a corresponding biblical affirmation next to it. For example, we wrote, "We are scared to face all of our debt." Corresponding biblical affirmation: "Do not fear, for I have redeemed you; I have summoned you by name; you are mine" (Isaiah 43:1b). We studied Isaiah 43 when the Lord comforts the Israelites when they were under afflictions. He promised deliverance from Babylon, that He would be present in the midst of their affliction, and that He would protect them. Facing your financial fears is a spiritual process. Isaiah 43:1 says, "But now, this is what the Lord says—he who created you, Jacob, he who formed you, Israel: "Do not fear, for I have redeemed you; I have summoned you by name; you are mine." The Lord called the Israelites by name because of His love and intimate relationship with them. God had designated them to be His people. God has called you by name.

2 Timothy 1:7 says, "For the Spirit God gave us does not make us timid, but gives us power, love and self-discipline." You do not have to be fearful because God has redeemed you and equipped you with power, love, and self-control to overcome your fears. Acknowledge your fears and write each one of them down. Write a corresponding biblical affirmation next to each of your fears. Focus on your small victories rather than your fears. Identify your fears and trust God to help you to face and conquer every one of your fears. Facing your financial fears arms you with a plan of action to fight your financial battles.

Prayer:

Today, Lord, I will not be afraid or discouraged about my finances because I am Yours and my finances belong to You. I will not be afraid to stay committed to this forty-day financial renewal experience until the end. Replace my fears with faith. Amen.

Reading:

Isaiah 43:1: "But now, this is what the Lord says—he who created you, Jacob, he who formed you, Israel: 'Do not fear, for I have redeemed you; I have summoned you by name; you are mine.'"

Application:

List all of your financial fears. Write a corresponding scripture next to each fear.

DAY 32
Obedience Is Better than Sacrifice

Obedience is a key component to showing our love and commitment to God. God wants us to obey Him. Our obedience to God proves our love for Him (1 John 5:2–3). It demonstrates to Him that we trust him, and it opens up many opportunities to receive all of the blessings that He has in store for us (John 13:17). When God gave Ken the vision over thirteen years ago to start the Hallelujah House Outreach Ministry Center, a nonprofit organization that provides resources to people in the community who are in need, he did it out of his obedience to God. At the time, I was pregnant with Kennedi. Prophetically, we would end up needing some of the same resources from the outreach ministry center a few months after the tragic birth of Kennedi.

We had people from all walks of life to donate to the vision because they could see that it was an opportunity to help many people. Regretfully, there were some people who did not understand God's vision to have an outreach ministry center in the community; thus, they did not support it. When Saul disobeyed God by not sacrificing the animals as the Lord had commanded, his loyalty was to the people instead of the Lord. The Lord saw his disobedience and repented for making Saul a king (v. 11). Many of us have been disobedient when it comes to giving to our churches and supporting our leader's vision. One of the main reasons some Christians struggle with giving to their church is because they cannot see God's vision for the church and "where there is no vision the people perish" (Proverbs 29:18).

God gives His vision for the church to the pastor through time in prayer because the pastor is the shepherd (1 Peter 5:2). Your pastor needs your support. God calls pastors to their churches for a specific purpose. They are given a vision to grow the church physical, spiritually, and financially. They cannot do it by themselves; they need the entire body to participate in order to be an effective and successful church. It is your spiritual responsibility to support your pastor's vision. We pray that you will see your pastor's or church leader's vision for your church and support them wholeheartedly. It will take some sacrifice. When you sacrifice for God and give to God's kingdom building program, He will bless you beyond measures.

The churches that are successful is because the people bought into the pastor's vision. As leaders, we have learned firsthand that people typically buy into the pastor first before they buy into the pastor's vision. Pastors must develop relationships with their congregations in order to build trust. If trust is not developed, the people will never buy into the vision. People typically do not join churches that do not support their pastor. And they certainly will not give to rebellious churches. In fact, people tend to run from controversial churches. Therefore, we feel that it is important to create a church environment that is safe for people to get to know each other and grow. Ken has strategically developed small groups within our church that allow opportunities for people to connect with one another and to build relationships. If you are a new pastor to a congregation, consider building strong relationships with your members a top priority before you make any radical changes.

If you are a member who has just received a new pastor, try not to prejudge your pastor. Make a deliberate effort to build a relationship with him/her. Do not undermine the pastor's vision. When you undermine your pastor's vision, it negatively affects God's kingdom building process. You will not reach your full potential until you learn to be obedient to your pastor's vision for the church. If you are a member who is struggling with obedience, you need to examine your heart. What is causing you to rebel against godly authority? What is causing you not to trust? What are you afraid of? Churches thrive on support from the Body of Christ. Make a commitment today to support your pastor's or church leader's vision.

Prayer:

Today, Lord, I want to be obedient. Show me Your ways. Bind the enemy from tempting me to hold back my tithes that is owed to You each month. Give me the strength to stand firm in the midst of fear and doubt. Help me to be obedient so that I will receive the desires of my heart. Amen.

Reading:

1 Samuel 15:22: "But Samuel replied: 'Does the Lord delight in burnt offerings and sacrifices as much as in obeying the Lord? To obey is better than sacrifice, and to heed is better than the fat of rams.'"

Application:

What is your attitude toward obedience to God, to your pastor and/ or others in authority? What can you do to support your pastor's/ leader's vision?

DAY 33
Sacrifice a Thanks Offering

God is delighted when His children offer to him spiritual sacrifices. In 2 Samuel 24:24, David came to offer a sacrifice and prayer for the removal of a plague on Israel. David understood what it meant to sacrifice a thanks offering. He knew that he had to give up something in order for his prayer to be answered. A thanks offering gives you an opportunity to glorify God with your giving as you give Him thanks for the many blessings that He has bestowed upon your life. God knows you cannot pay Him for the unlimited blessings that He has provided for you. Thanksgiving in the Bible is giving thanks to God for *everything* that He has given humankind including life, food, drinks (Acts 17:25).

Pastors have a sacred assignment that should be respected and honored. God has entrusted the pastor to lead His flock. Pastors are like medical doctors in that they are spiritual doctors who have been put in charge of the spiritual health of God's people. The job of a medical doctor is to provide preventive care to preserve life and to prevent an early death. Spiritual doctors (pastors) preaches "the wages of sin is death" (Romans 6:23) and "that everyone who believes may have eternal life in God" (John 3:15). A medical doctor prescribes medicine and the spiritual doctor prescribes the Word of God. Pastor's appreciation service is a special time that congregations set aside each year to honor their pastors for their hard work, dedication, and blessings that they give to the Body of Christ. This typically involves each member to give a special gift offering to the pastor.

Pastors and their families live under high demands and pressure. We live our lives in the public with the entire congregation and community watching our every move. We are expected to have the "perfect families" and to "live perfect lives." As you know, no one on earth is perfect and we certainly are not perfect—far from it. Unfortunately, when we do not live up to the unrealistic expectations, it can be disappointing and devastating to some people in the church. Now, that is a lot of pressure for pastors and their families. God wants you to honor your pastor. Paul said according to First Timothy 5:17, "The elders who direct the affairs of the church well are worthy of double honor, especially those whose work is preaching and teaching." Remember, the pastor and his or her spouse are partners in marriage as well as ministry. Thus, when the pastor suffers, the entire family is impacted.

You should not base your giving on your pastor's personal assets, i.e., his/her home, car, clothes, etc., rather base it on his/her works and what he/she has done for you and the church. Your sacrificial thanks offering to your pastor is your offering that expresses your gratitude for the special blessings that your pastor has provided in your spiritual journey. It could be the help that your pastor and family need to get through a personal financial hardship. It may cost you something to give, but it is worth it. Ken and I have decided to give our personal thanks offering at least once a year. It may come in a form a monetary gift to our church, or it may be in the form of a service to our congregation. We may write a check for $500 to $1,000, or we might buy lunch for our entire congregation. One year we had a Membership Appreciation Day. This was a time for us to say thank you to our entire congregation for everything they had ever done for us and the church. After church one Sunday, we literally served each member fish dinners.

One year we gave each member gourmet candy and a thanksgiving card. Another year we bought each member fresh Georgia peaches. Several church members were surprised and told us that they had never seen such a thing. It is the most exuberating feeling to give a thanks offering unto God's people. We encourage you to take the time to sacrifice a thanks offering for your pastor or church leader who sacrificially gives of his/her life so that you and others might be saved. This offering goes specifically to your pastor, not to your church. Your pastor and his/her family deserve this kind of appreciation. Make a sacrificial thanks offering today!

Prayer:

Today, Lord, I will sacrifice a thank offering to you. This offering is to show You gratitude for the gifts that surround me, for Your blessings, for covering me and my family, and for the joy you've placed in my heart. Amen.

Read:

2 Samuel 24:24: "But the king replied to Araunah, 'No, I insist on paying you for it. I will not sacrifice to the Lord my God burnt offerings that cost me nothing.' So David bought the threshing floor and the oxen and paid fifty shekels of silver for them."

Application:

What are you willing to give up in order to give this sacrificial offering today?

DAY 34
A Season of Renewal

Solomon shares with us that life is all about timing in Ecclesiates 3:1–15. In his attempt to understand the true meaning of life, he sees that good times and bad times come to all, and the process repeats itself in each coming season. He concludes that the wise man will understand this process and prepare himself for life's trials and triumph. Every person on earth has to go through different seasons in life in order to grow and mature. In each season, you will experience many life changes. You must prepare for each of your seasons of life just as you do with the four seasons of the year: spring, summer, autumn, and winter. Your clothes must change with each of the seasons in order to live comfortably in the different seasons. To be honest, Kennedi's illness and death seemed like a four-year-long tornado season.

Tornado season is typically in the spring because most of them are in the months of March through June. They are violent rotating winds with speed up to 300 mph that comes from a thunderstorm. When they hit the ground, the mass destruction can be so severe that they can literally destroy homes, large buildings, uproot trees, and throw vehicles miles away. One of our dear friends who miraculously survived a 2015 tornado in Rowlett, Texas compared the sound of the tornado to that of a freight train. While taking cover, she listened helplessly as her entire home was demolished by the tornado. She described how she could literally hear the tornado tearing apart her home. Each time she shares her experience, we can see the trauma in her face as she relives one of the worst moments in her life. The EF4 tornado blew through the cities of Garland, Rowlett and Sunnyvale and killed at least eight people that year. According to the Weather Service, the tornado had winds up to 180 mph.

Just like a tornado, our lives seemed to be spinning out of control. It seemed like we were being hit with all of the debris of life. Through our tragedies, we learned that there will be many experiences in life that we cannot control. Daniel 2:21, "He changes times and seasons; he deposes kings and raises up others. He gives wisdom to the wise and knowledge to the discerning." Our tragic situation caused massive emotional, spiritual, mental, and financial destruction. Our lives were so chaotic that we do not remember some experiences; it is a blur. But our spiritual and financial journey helped us to seek God's guidance as we dealt with the changing seasons. After our personal storm, we had to go through a cleanup and recovery process, which is the essence of a financial renewal process.

We consider our financial renewal as a new season of life that propelled us toward a new life, new home, new career, new attitude, new thought process, new perspective on life, and a new sense of being. We praise God even in the midst of our most destructive storms because we know that He will help us get through it. Psalm 28:7 says, "The Lord is my strength and my shield; my heart trusts in him, and he helps me. My heart leaps for joy, and with my song I praise him." Always remember that God is in control of your seasons. Your seasons of life may change, but God never changes. He is the same yesterday and today and forever (Hebrews 13:8).

Each new season introduces a change in your life. God wants you to have financial peace during this season of your life. At the end of the day, your financial peace comes from your dependence on God. In every season, you will either be going into a storm, already in a storm, or coming out of a storm. No matter what season you are in, you can choose how you will respond. Learn a positive lesson from each season of your life. Your financial goals, income, and expenses will most likely change with each season. Know that God is working things out for your good in every season of your life. Allow your seasons of life to build your character and strength for the next season.

Prayer:

Today, Lord, my life is in Your hands. My times are in your hands. My finances are in Your hands. In this season of financial renewal, I see the next stage of my life as one in which to grow, learn, and prosper. Amen.

Reading:

Ecclesiastes 3:1. "There is a time for everything, and a season for every activity under the heavens."

Application:

What season are you in at this time in your life? What do you need to let go of before you enter your new season?

DAY 35
Being Wonderfully Made

Psalm 139:14 says, "I praise you because I am fearfully and wonderfully made; your works are wonderful, I know that full well." It is clear that God created us in such wisdom, power, and love so that we can honor Him and glorify His name. Every person in the Body of Christ is an individual piece of art, and God is the Master Artist. He uses every life experience-good, bad, and indifferent to create His individual masterpieces. Your existence has nothing to do with you. Your life is predestined, and the only reason why you have survived this long is because your destiny has to line up with what God already sees for your life. You have to grasp the vision for your life. The only way you can grasp God's vision for your life is to be in the spirit. God's vision for your life has to move from your spirit to your mind, and that is when you experience life transformation and manifestation by the renewal of your mind.

We knew that God did not make a mistake when He allowed us to go through the trials with Kennedi and the subsequent financial problems. He used our situation and circumstances so that we would have a testimony of His power and anointing. It is a part of our destiny. God is using everything that you have gone through, are going through right now, and will go through to create your destiny. You are a masterpiece being wonderfully made by God. God is painting the perfect picture of your life using the following five Cs of a masterpiece:

Cost–a masterpiece is very costly. As an accountant and consultant, I have had an opportunity to work for some wealthy people who pay a lot of money for masterpieces just so they can display them in the privacy of their homes. In fact, I had a client who collected art pieces from all around the world. She had invested in so many pieces that she ran out of wall space to hang them. Therefore, she started leaning them on the wall down her hallways. I often thought about how only a few of her friends and family got an opportunity to experience the beauty of her art pieces. They just collected dust. The last time I calculated her net worth, her art collection was worth well over a half a million dollars. Just like it cost my client to display the beautiful masterpieces in her home, it cost Jesus to take our sins upon the cross and die for them. Isaiah 53:5 says, "But he was pierced for our transgressions, he was crushed for our iniquities; the punishment that brought us peace was on him, and by his wounds we are healed." You are valuable to God!

Credible–a masterpiece is discussed and argued for its credibility as a work of art. As Christians, our Christianity is founded on the resurrection of Jesus Christ from the dead. When you identify yourself as a Christian, that means you are living a Christ-centered life. Consequently, you will always have people watching to see if you are a credible witness. First Peter 2:21 says, "For to this you have been called, because Christ also suffered for you, leaving you an example, so that you might follow in his steps." The bible tells us that every believer must share the Gospel. (Mark 16:15) To be a credible witness, you should always be prepared to share the Gospel of Jesus Christ.

Critique–a masterpiece has to be critiqued. Before a masterpiece can ever be put in the hall of fame or a museum, it first has to go through the hall of critics. The critics have to see if they can criticize it. When it stands the critics, then it is finally taken to the hall of fame. Most people do not like criticism because it makes you feel like someone is pointing out your weaknesses, which causes you to be defensive. However, constructive criticism helps to build and strengthen you, so be humble and listen intentionally when someone is critiquing you. Proverbs 11:2 says, "When pride comes, then comes disgrace, but with the humble is wisdom." You should embrace constructive criticism because it not only helps you to see the areas in your life that need improvement, but it also reminds you that it is okay to have imperfections.

Created for a purpose–the purpose of a masterpiece is to communicate the artist's ideas, vision and inner expression of creativity. Ephesians 2:10 says "For we are God's handiwork, created in Christ Jesus to do good works, which God prepared in advance for us to do." God created you for a specific purpose. He wants to use you in His kingdom to make a difference.

Colorful story–a masterpiece is colorful and has special qualities that make it special and attractive. Each one of us have a colorful story. When you share your story, it gives God the glory because your story is His-story. Just like a beautiful painting, your life is filled will a mixture of colors. Some days will be blue, filled with sadness. Some days will be gold, filled with the spirit. Some days will be gray, filled with confusion. Some days will be red, filled with love. Some days will be pink, filled with happiness. God uses all of the "colors" in our lives to make the perfect combination of colors for His masterpiece. Psalm 119:46 says, "I will also speak of your testimonies before kings and shall not be put to shame." Dare to share your story. Your story can help so many people. You are God's masterpiece.

You are God's unique design – a masterpiece created in His image. God wants you to live in abundant wealth so you can bless others and establish His covenant. He has equipped you with the resources that you need to be financially blessed. You must grasp His vision for your life in order to experience the manifestation of wealth.

Prayer:

Today, Lord, I praise You because I am fearfully and wonderfully made. You made everything beautiful including me. I will walk boldly in your anointing knowing that You are King of Kings. Amen.

Reading:

Psalm 139:14. "I praise you because I am fearfully and wonderfully made; your works are wonderful, I know that full well."

Application:

How do you feel about yourself? What can you do to bless yourself today?

DAY 36
My Grace Is Sufficient

All of us have flaws, weaknesses, trials, etc. However, all people do not deal with them the same. Some people spend most of their lives beating themselves up because they are perfectionists. Perfectionists believe that everything must be perfect at all times, not allowing any room for error, obstacles, and detour. Well, we know that life will not be perfect. There will always be pessimist who see life from "Why me," "What if," and "Woe unto me" perspectives. Their lives are filled with negativity. In 2 Corinthians 12:9, Paul says, "But he said to me, 'My grace is sufficient for you, for my power is made perfect in weakness.' Therefore, I will boast all the more gladly about my weaknesses, so that Christ's power may rest on me." Paul had a thorn of some sort that caused him to be afflicted. But, God was right there with Paul to help him get through his affliction.

When God told Paul, "My grace is sufficient for you," He was implying that His favor was all Paul needed to fulfill his calling to take the gospel to the Gentiles (Acts 9:15, Ephesians 3:0). God's blessing was enough for Paul to live with his affliction for a long period of time in spite of whatever physical, spiritual, or emotional pain he was experiencing. The word "grace" means that in our human weakness Christ is able to perfect His strength. Grace is God's undeserved favor, His love and mercy given to us. Ken and I have discovered in the midst of our darkest moments that the grace of God is with us. God's blessing was enough for us to make it through our spiritual and emotional pain, no matter how long that pain existed.

God's grace was enough to sustain us until He determined when the pain should end. There were times when our negative thoughts creeped up. Some days I doubted God's favor over my life. I remember asking God, "Are you punishing me for some of the sins that I have committed in my life?" Ken reminded me that "Christ was pierced for our transgressions and crushed for our iniquities" (Isaiah 53:5). God's Word gave me comfort. What is your attitude about money and your pattern of spending? By now, during this financial renewal, your financial future should look so much brighter. Answer the following questions to determine your financial personality:

1. Is it easier for you to control your spending?
2. Have you saved any money during this financial renewal process?
3. Have you been able to stick with your budget?
4. Have you refrained from making any major purchases in the last thirty days?
5. Have you paid all of your bills on time within the last thirty days?
6. Do you use cash more than you use credit?
7. Are you more confident about your finances?
8. Have you increased your giving during this – financial renewal process?

If you answered "yes" to most of the questions, you are growing financially. You are a change agent. You made a choice to change your mind about your financial future. Your commitment to the process has opened doors for you to accomplish your financial goals. There may be some areas that you feel weak, but God is much closer than you think. His power is made perfect in your weakness. You can find God's grace through your prayers, meditation, studying His Word, worshipping, and fellowshipping with other believers. Your "thorns", whatever they are, are meant to make you stronger. Just like Paul, God is right there with you to help you get through your afflictions. It is our prayer that this book has encouraged you to trust God with your finances so you can experience financial victory.

Prayer:

Today, Lord, reveal my "thorn" to me and what You are trying to teach me through that "thorn". Give me strength to get through my financial struggles and setbacks so that I can receive financial victory. I release every thorn to You that is hindering me from financial victory. Amen.

Read:

2 Corinthians 12:9: "But he said to me, My grace is sufficient for you, for my power is made perfect in weakness. Therefore, I will boast all the more gladly about my weaknesses, so that Christ's power may rest on me."

Application:

What "thorn" (obstacle) keeps you from experiencing all that God has for you?

DAY 37
Living in the Overflow

Our home is a lakeside property that sits on Lake Lewisville. We typically have a little of the lake water to overflow into our backyard, which forms a nice small pond. Every now and then, we might see a few fish and black water moccasins (creepy!) swimming in the pond. It is a beautiful view from our windows. This is one of the main reasons why we really wanted to buy the house over ten years ago. But in May of 2015, it rained for several days straight causing the water levels to get extremely high. Every day we would watch the water in our backyard get higher and higher. The houses that sat directly on the lake experienced major flooding. Their entire backyards were covered with water.

Many of the streets in our community were blocked off due to flooding. The water in our backyard eventually got so high it was just a few feet from our back door. We started to get very concerned because it was the first time we had ever seen it get that high in ten years. The Lewisville Lake spillway became a big tourist attraction. We even made the news. The officials assured us that we were not in any danger of our homes being flooded. I am convinced that if it would have rained a few more days, we would have had to evacuate. We thank God that the rain finally stopped before that happened.

The word overflow is defined as excess or surplus, not able to be accommodated by an available space. That is the type of overflow that God wants us to experience in our lives.

God is a God of overflow. He gives us all that we need and more. Ken is very demonstrative. Every time he preaches, he uses some type of unique demonstration to drive his points in his sermons. This is perfect for visual style learners like myself. Visual learners tend to learn better with visual objects, images and pictures. One of my personal favorite sermons that he preaches is "Living in God's Overflow." He uses a glass as a representation of Christians, a pitcher as a representation of God, and the water inside the pitcher represents the Holy Spirit. First, he pours the water in the glass until it is half-full to represent how some Christians are living half-empty spiritual lives. Then he pours into another glass until the water spills over the top onto the floor. This represents Christians living in the overflow of abundance—overflow of financial blessings, overflow of love, overflow of the Holy Spirit, etc.

In Romans 15:13, Paul's prayer is for every believer to experience hope. "Now may the God of hope fill you with all joy and peace in believing so that you will abound in hope by the power of the Holy Spirit." Paul's source of living in the overflow was his hope in God. When he referred to God of hope, he is saying that God is the giver of hope and hope rests on God's promises. He promises that He will "open the floodgates of heaven and pour out so much blessing that you will not have room enough for it" (Malachi 3:10). He promises that if you "Give, and it will be given to you. A good measure, pressed down, shaken together and running over, will be poured into your lap" (Luke 6:38).

There are not enough Christians living in this type of overflow. They are barely making ends meet and spend a lot of time worrying about their finances. It takes faith to receive God's overflow of blessings. Galatians 3:14 says, "He redeemed us in order that the blessing given to Abraham might come to the Gentiles through Christ Jesus, so that by faith we might receive the promise of the Spirit." You must believe in the promises of God and know that there is nothing too impossible with God (Luke 1:37). You have been called to live in the overflow of God's blessings. When you live in the overflow, it will change your life.

Prayer:

Today, Lord, I want to enter into Your overflow of blessings. I will keep my eyes on Your promises, and not my limitations. I want to experience the overflowing abundance that You want me to enjoy. Fill me with more of Your love, joy, and peace. Amen.

Read:

Romans 15:13: "May the God of hope fill you with all joy and peace as you trust in him, so that you may overflow with hope by the power of the Holy Spirit."

Application:

What does it mean to you to live in the overflow of God's blessings?

DAY 38
Pray Without Ceasing

We cannot stress enough the importance of prayer in your daily walk with God. Prayer literally changes everything. Prayer helps make "all things work together for good of those who love Him, who have been called according to His purpose" (Romans 8:26–28). In Thessalonians 5:16–17, Paul is very specific about the things that he expects Christians to do continually. Paul says we should rejoice, pray, and give thanks to God. Ken and I have prayed through many life trials, and God has always come through for us every time. In fact, we have faced several family crises during the time we wrote this book. Even through our crisis, we had a "peace that surpasses understanding" (Philippians 4:7) because we kept our eyes on Christ instead of our problems. We kept reminding ourselves how our faith in God got us through our crisis with Kennedi. If He did it then, He would certainly do it again. There is nothing impossible for God.

We even experienced a medical situation with Ken that came as a complete surprise. He had a slight swelling on the left side of his chest. At first we thought it was cancer. It was protruding and very painful for him. We immediately called our primary-care physician to make an appointment. Then we began to pray for healing before we received the results from our physician. We called our prayer partners, prayer warriors, and intercessors to pray with us. We prayed for guidance, wisdom, and peace about our situation. We started thanking God for His many blessings, for protecting us and for using us to be living testimonies. Ken was given a referral to go to the cancer center for X-rays and testing. We had to wait for several days for Ken to see an oncologist and to get the results of his tests. A few days later, we learned that Ken did not have cancer. We shouted, danced, and praised as we thanked God for a great report!

We knew that through continual prayer, God would prevail and get the glory. We are so thankful to God that when we retreat to our prayer closets, bombarding heaven with our earthly concerns, God always speaks in powerful ways. This forty-day financial renewal has focused on praying every day and petitioning God daily for guidance and direction for financial victory. Prayer is birthed out of our obedience to God. Obedience is doing God's will and keeping His commandments. James 2:12 tells us, "Speak and act as those who are going to be judged by the law that gives freedom." You may be praying for a financial blessing to get out of debt or to provide for your family. Your obedience will produce a standard of reliability, accountability, and dependability.

If you are new to prayer, consider getting a prayer partner. Participate in your church prayer line where there are others assembled together in prayer. If your local church does not have a church prayer line, call another church's prayer line so you can partner with other prayer warriors. A strong prayer life will give you the strength to survive the day-to-day stressors of life. We encourage you to continue praying every day even after you finish this book. Refer back to it as needed, take notes, highlight things that specifically spoke to you. If you do not have a prayer partner, ask God to send you someone who you can pray with on a regular basis and be accountable to. We ask that you continue to pray for us, as we continue to do God's will for our lives.

Prayer:

Today, Lord, even though I am almost finished with my forty-day financial renewal experience, I will continue to pray without ceasing. I want to continue to experience the joy of uniting in prayer with You for the rest of my life. Strengthen me in areas that I need improvement. Amen.

Read:

1 Thessalonians 5:16–17: "Rejoice always, pray without ceasing."

Application:

How can you improve your prayer life? (List specific areas of improvement.)

DAY 39
An Abundant Life

Some Christians vacillate in their everyday lives to live according to the world's standard while trying to adhere to God's standards. Most of us want to live the American dream, a life of financial stability that includes a husband/wife, a good-paying job, 2.5 kids, a dog, a big house with a picket fence, late-model cars in your garages, and able to take exotic vacations anytime you want. More and more people are finding the American dream harder and unrealistic to achieve due to financial hardships. God wants you to live an abundant life. Throughout the Bible, we witness God's promise to bless people. An abundant life is not about us accumulating a lot of assets. It is more about receiving from God all that He has for us. An abundant life is only achieved through Jesus. The abundant life does not mean having an abundance of material goods; it is living a righteous life in Jesus Christ. Satan tries to destroy us through materialism, consumerism, competition, greed, selfishness, and strife, which blinds us from living the abundant life that God promised. In John 10:10, the Lord identifies Satan as the deceiver, thief, murderer, and destroyer.

Ephesians 1:3 says, "Blessed be the God and Father of our Lord Jesus Christ, who hath blessed us with all spiritual blessings in heavenly places in Christ." You are blessed so that you can be a blessing to others. But before you can truly be a blessing to others, you have to understand the context of what it means to live an abundant life. Your financial renewal comes as a result of living a God-centered life and biblical stewardship. A part of biblical stewardship is planning your financial future. We have met many people in the Body of Christ who have entered into retirement age without adequate retirement income. As a result, they spend the latter parts of their lives in anxiety, depression, and stress. Most people who are sixty-five and older look forward to getting their Social Security benefits. Social Security is a governmental program financed by employees and employers. It was intended to be used as a supplementary income to your retirement income, not as the primary source of income. However, many people use it as their sole source of retirement income. They are living off Social Security income, which is barely enough to cover their basic living expenses. Retirement should be a time of rest, relaxation, and rewards for a lifetime of hard work and sacrifice.

Your main source of retirement income should include retirement programs offered by your employer, personal retirement plans, and/or annuities. Retirement planning is imperative for financial security. To learn more about planning for your retirement, you should consult with a professional financial planner or advisor. People are living longer and retiring sooner than ever before. In fact, currently our oldest member at North Park C. M. E. Church is 105 years old. The earlier you start planning how you would like to spend your time during retirement, the better it is for you to have enough money to live at retirement age. You hold the keys to your abundant life. God has already promised you an abundant life. All you have to do is unlock the door and walk in victory. I am reminded of a time when I pulled up to our home after a long, stressful day at work only to find that the key to my front door was gone from my key ring. Somehow a single key had fallen off of my key ring. The entire drive home, I had fantasized about getting home to relax under my favorite blanket. Ken was out of town, and my spare key was locked in the house. I walked around the house to check all doors and windows in hopes that we may have inadvertently left one of them open. Unfortunately, everything was locked. I was so desperate to get in our home that I considered kicking in the door or breaking a window. I dreaded the call to a locksmith because I knew that they would most likely charge me an enormous amount of money to re-key the lock and/or create a new key.

It took the locksmith about two hours to arrive. Then it took him another hour to create a key. I grew more anxious and frustrated as I waited to get in my home. He finally finished the job and handed me an invoice for $280. Reluctantly I had to pay the price for not having my key to unlock the door. As I unloaded my bags from my car, I noticed a shiny silver key on the floor of the driver's side. It was my house key. Somehow it had fallen off my key ring when I had gotten out of my car. I had a feeling of disgust knowing that I had wasted so much time and money for a single key that was readily available to unlock my door. Looking back, I realized that God revealed a very profound principle to me: many people do not realize that they already hold the key to an abundant life. Jesus is your key to an abundant life. He is always with you even when you cannot see Him or trace Him. Your key to an abundant life lies in the promises of God. Discover the blessings in the power of His abundance and walk through the "door of victory."

Prayer:

Today, Lord, according Your Word, the thief comes to steal, kill, and destroy everything good in my life. He wants to destroy my job, my finances, my family, my health, my finances, my relationships, especially my relationship with You. Give me the power to resist every attack and to overcome every strategy the devil will try to use against me! Protect me, Lord. Amen.

Reading:

John 10:10: "The thief comes only to steal and kill and destroy; I have come that they may have life, and have it to the full."

Application:

What steps can you take now to prepare for your retirement income?

DAY 40
Financial Renewal Testimony

Praise God! You have made it to day 40 of your financial renewal process! You should be proud of yourself. You have completed this journey filled with prayer, praise, conviction, restoration, and renewal. We are sure that you thought about giving up along the way, but you stayed committed to the process. We have gone through this financial-renewal process on several occasions so we know that it can be challenging. We have shared this great experience with our family, church family, and friends; thus, we know that this can be a life-changing, transformative experience. We have heard so many amazing testimonies about unexpected blessings and financial breakthroughs. This book is our personal testimony of tragedy and triumph. It took a tragedy to catapult us to a place of healing and renewal. We are all one tragedy away from losing it all. It is only by God's grace and mercy that we have survived certain experiences. "What the devil meant for evil, God meant if for our good. (Genesis 50:20) We believe that the enemy wanted to destroy us, but God used our trials to build us up.

We pray that something we have shared has inspired and empowered you to trust God and to know that life is all about processes. Nothing happens overnight. Most of the successful people that we know had to go through some type of trial in order to get to their level of success. Successful people usually fail more often than others do; they succeed primarily because they just won't quit trying. It is certain that any person who has been successful is also a person who has failed. [3] We realize that failure is a very important part of success. We have learned to use our failures as stepping stones for personal growth and maturity. We are always excited to hear about God's amazing grace. We thank God for giving us the courage and for using us as living testimonies to share some of our most intimate experiences with you. We all have a personal testimony of faith. Our testimonies are well-designed personal testimonies of faith that can permeate the hearts of those who hear it. It is our ability to relate how the Lord has specifically worked in our lives to anoint us for His service. The purpose of sharing our testimony is to demonstrate His miraculous intervention and to work through our specific experiences. It gives us an opportunity to describe how the Spirit leads, guides, molds, and shapes us into mature Christians. Most people want to know that you believe in the power of the Holy Spirit and how He has affected your life. Sharing your personal testimony allows you to share the Gospel of Jesus Christ and to connect personally with other believers.

Each time we go through the forty-day financial renewal we experience a mighty move of God. I will not attempt to name every blessing, however I will name a few that stand out in my mind. In September 2015, we introduced the forty-day financial renewal to our church family and started it together. Each day we read scriptures, prayed, and discussed

---

[3] 2000 In Secret Sources of Power: Rediscovering Biblical Power Points, by T.F. Tenney and Tommy Tenney, 55 Shippensburg: Destiny Image Publishers, Inc.

our finances on our church prayer conference line. Some of our members shared powerful testimonies about how they received unexpected checks in the mail, new jobs, salary increases, college scholarships, and much more. I personally received a salary increase on my job during the forty-day renewal experience. Ken's speaking and preaching engagements doubled during the forty-day financial renewal. Tithes and offering increased at our church. We witnessed a renewal of our personal finances.

We believe that God has blessed you and given you a powerful testimony during these last forty days as well. Our prayer is that this book has given you a fresh start and a renewed perspective about your covenant with God and your personal finances.

In 1 Peter 3:15, Peter makes it clear that Christians should be prepared to give a reason for the hope that we have. People are going to see a change in you and your financial future. Quite naturally, they are going to ask you about your change. This is your opportunity to share your financial renewal experiences and your reason for hope. We pray that you will share your testimony. Please share your personal testimonies with us at 40dayfinancialrenewal@gmail.com. We would also like for you to follow us on Twitter: @hollingshedt14 (Tanesha) and klhollingshed7 (Kenneth) for updates, new products and services. Thank you for taking this journey and for trusting God in the process.

Prayer:

Today, Lord, I thank you for giving me the strength to make it to day 40 of this financial renewal experience. Allow me to be a living testimony that my financial breakthroughs come as a result of living by your biblical principles. I pray that my life and finances says something to someone about Your power and Your provision. Amen.

Read:

1 Peter 3:15: "But in your hearts revere Christ as Lord. Always be prepared to give an answer to everyone who asks you to give the reason for the hope that you have. But do this with gentleness and respect."

Application:

What has God done for you during this financial renewal experience? (Give your testimony) What have you learned during this financial renewal experience?

RENEWAL IN HEAVEN

I had suffered from guilt for several months after our beloved daughter, Kennedi died. I kept reliving the fact that she had been sleeping in our bedroom ever since she was released from the NICCU up until I talked Ken into allowing her to sleep in her own bed. Ken and I were not sleeping much because she would cry and have severe seizures all night long. As her mother, I felt so helpless when I watched her suffer. Her neurologist had increased her dose of valium so she and everyone else in the house could sleep during the night. If she slept, we all slept. We were always afraid to let her sleep alone because we thought she might choke on her own saliva or have a seizure so violent that it would take her life. After her last increase of valium, I literally begged Ken to allow Kennedi to sleep in her own bed so we could get back to a normal life. We were both going to work each day exhausted. Against his better judgment, Ken finally agreed to allow her to sleep in her own bed, but only if I agreed to get monitors for our beds. We purchased monitors, and everything seemed to be going smoothly. If we heard her cry at night, we would immediately get up to care for her.

The day before she left us, she and I had slept on the couch snuggled together all day. That night, the entire family watched television together. I will never forget the look of peace on her face and that soft grin that she had before Ken put her in her bed. It was as if she were trying to tell us something. It would be the last night we would ever see her alive. After her death, I kept having a series of thoughts: *Why didn't I understand her expressions? I did not have a chance to tell her bye. I did not give her my normal good night hug and kiss. I did not tell her how much I loved her. If she would have been in the bed with me, I could have saved her life.* I cried myself asleep most nights. I looked like I was living a normal life on the outside, but I was suffering on the inside. My heart hurt, my stomach hurt, I had migraines. She kept coming back trying to communicate with me. I kept seeing visions of her with that dried-up blood on the side of her mouth and on her pink shirt, just like the morning we found her. She kept trying to talk to me, but I could not understand what she was saying to me. She even followed me to our new home and on my job. I thought I was losing my mind.

I felt like I was being haunted by Kennedi. I continued to see a therapist on a weekly basis. My therapist diagnosed me with posttraumatic stress disorder (PTSD), so she continued to prescribe me different medicines to help me. But nothing seemed to help me with the grief and Kennedi's sudden appearances. I pleaded with God daily to allow me to see Kennedi one more time so that I could apologize, hug her, and put closure to her death. About a year after we moved into our new home, I had an out-of-body experience that changed my life forever. I normally do not share this story because I know that people will come up with different logic and psychology in order to rationalize it in their own minds. I am going to get out of my comfort zone and share my supernatural experience with you. I pray that this story blesses you. Here it goes.

One night after I went to bed, the Lord answered my prayers and allowed me to see and talk to Kennedi. I had been begging Him to allow me one opportunity to hold her and put closure to her death. As a result, He "arranged" a meeting. I woke up in heaven. I still had on my pajamas that I wore to bed, and I was barefooted. I was standing in what appeared to be acres and acres of nothing but green land. The grass was perfect and felt like cotton under my feet. I knew I was in heaven because I could feel God's anointing. I did not see any buildings, no "pearly gates," no "streets of gold," no "white doves" flying, no "rainbow," nothing but a big beautiful tree in the middle of nowhere that stood about one-half mile directly in front of me.

The closer I walked toward the tree, the more I could see a small silhouette of a person standing next to it. Once I got close enough, I realized it was Kennedi, so I ran to her, picked her up, hugged and kissed her. I was in disbelief! I cried tears of joy. Oh my god, she was so beautiful. Her skin was clear and radiant; she had this incredible glow. Her soft, wavy blackish-brown hair was combed back and had grown about midlevel down her back. I put her down and kneeled down so I could talk to her at eye level. Our conversation went as such: "Baby, I came to tell you that I am so sorry for not saving your life, I let you die. I love you so much. I miss you and I wish you were back with us." I broke down crying.

Kennedi said, "Mommy, I do not want to come back. I love my new home. I can walk, talk, I can see you better, and I do not hurt anymore. See, look at me!" With a big beautiful smile on her face, she started jumping up and down to show me how strong she was. "You did not let me die. Jesus came to get me and He was not going to let you save me."

I had never seen her smile like that. Most days she appeared to be uncomfortable, and often had a look of discomfort or a frown on her face.

I asked, "Why do you keep visiting me? It seems like you are trying to tell me something."

"I was trying to tell you not to be sad because I am happy with my new family here. And I love playing with them every day. They take care of me. But you could not hear me, Mommy. Tell Daddy not to be sad. I loved riding to school with him every day. I loved when he talked to me during our daily rides. Tell him that I love him."

As she talked to me, I kept thinking about how I could take her back with me. I could tell that my time with her was about to end soon. I wanted to run away with her.

"Please come back with me, Kennedi. I need you." I had a strong urgency to pick her up and start running, but I was too scared.

"Mommy, I cannot go with you. I have to stay here." She reached out her hand as if someone was reaching for her. I could tell that she sensed that I was about to attempt to take her.

I could not see anyone, but she looked as if she could see and hear things that I was not privy to. Whoever was communicating with her was leading her to another direction. I gave her another big kiss and a hug as I said, "bye-bye."

"Bye-bye, Mommy. Thank you for coming to see me. I am always with you. I love you."

I immediately woke up in my bed. I wept as I shared my out-of-body experience with Ken. He comforted me and softly said to me, "I believe you. Tell me all about it." We talked for the rest of the morning. Ken believes that if I had snatched Kennedi and ran with her, I probably would have died in my sleep that night because I would have gone against God's will. It was a frightening thought of the consequences that I would have faced if I had taken what belongs to God. Since that day, I have never seen anymore images or visions of Kennedi again. But every now and then, I know she is there because I can smell her or feel her presence. I have never had any more post-traumatic stress disorder symptoms, nor anxiety. I was instantaneously healed after my encounter in heaven. I no longer view life the same after that awesome experience. It was my spiritual healing and renewal in heaven. And based on that little part of heaven that I was privy to, I truly believe that our ultimate renewal is eternal life with God.

You are simply a manager of God's resources while you are here on earth. None of the resources that you spend so much time worrying about, stressing over, and chasing will make it into eternity with you. In Second Corinthians 5, The Apostle Paul writes his second letter to the Corinthians letting them know the reasons why they did not faint under their afflictions. It was mainly because of their expectations, desires, and assurance of happiness after death (v. 1-5). Then he apologizes for commending himself, and gives a good reason for his passion and diligence (v. 12-15). He mentions two things that are necessary in order to live a Christian life: renewal and reconciliation (v. 16-21). What unresolved matters are you facing at this moment? Pray for your healing and deliverance. Give it to God. It is through God that you can experience renewal and reconciliation.

ABOUT THE AUTHORS

TANESHA HOLLINGSHED is a native of Oklahoma, preacher's wife, mother, preacher, teacher, motivational and inspirational speaker, singer, and accountant. Behind her beautiful smile and humor is a story of tragedy and triumph. She has dedicated her life to helping others transform their lives and discover God's divine purpose for their lives. Tanesha has been a member of the Christian Methodist Episcopal Church for over seventeen years and has made great contributions to the kingdom. She is a praise-and-worship leader, local minister, women's book club ministry coordinator, national speaker, and conference facilitator. She is also instrumental in Christian education, Sunday school, Connectional Young Adult Ministry, A.W.E.S.O.M.E. Ministry (a teenage-girl ministry), and domestic violence ministry.

Tanesha is blessed to be able to combine her passion with her career. Recognized as a leading presenter in the field of business and personal finance, her message about the importance of financial literacy has resonated with many people nationally. Tanesha teaches business education classes including business, marketing, finance, business law, advertising and sales promotion, sports and entertainment, marketing, securities and investments, and professional communication to high school students in the Collin County public school district.

Prior to her career in education, she worked in Corporate America as an accountant and finance professional for over ten years. She earned her AAS in accounting from North Lake College, BBS in Accounting from Dallas Baptist University, and MA in teaching degree from Louisiana College. She holds Texas educator licensures in business education, marketing education, and speech. She is married to Kenneth, and they have two sons: Khaylen and Kingston. She enjoys cooking, exercising, reading, writing, hanging out at the lake or beach, and traveling.

REV. KENNETH L. HOLLINGSHED is a native of Georgia who has been in the ministry for over thirty-six years. He has served as the senior pastor of North Park Christian Methodist Episcopal (CME) Church in Dallas, Texas, since January 1998. He is a pastor, an evangelist, prophet, orator, trainer, teacher, visionary leader, social activist, licensed architect, and mentor to many pastors. He is the founder, president, and CEO of Hallelujah House Outreach Center Inc., a 501(c)(3) faith-based community center that reaches out to all of God's people. The ministry center houses several of the church's outreach ministries. Reverend Hollingshed has pastored many congregations and has led them to tremendous growth and kingdom expansion. He is one of the leading pastors in the CME denomination. He has served as a delegate to the General Conference (Connectional Church) for several years, Chairman of Evangelism & Spiritual Life since 2002 (Connectional Church), as well as in other leadership roles.

Rev. Hollingshed has been featured on the Fox 4 TV show, *Insights* and has made several Christian radio appearances informing the community of countless outreach programs and community-empowering projects that have reached thousands for the kingdom.

Rev. Hollingshed holds a BA in architectural engineering, BA in theology, MA in business organization and design planning. He is a graduate of United States Army Chaplain Center and School. He and Tanesha have been married for eighteen years and they have two sons: Khaylen and Kingston. He loves to read, watch movies, and fine dining.

APPENDIX
List of Consumer Advocates

Government Agencies:

United States Department of Agriculture: www.usda.gov
Consumer Product Safety Commission: www.cpsc.gov
Environmental Protection Agency: www.epa.gov
Federal Trade Commission: www.ftc.gov
Food and Drug Administration: www.fda.gov
Health and Human Services: www.hhs.gov
Housing and Urban Development: www.hud.gov
National Institutes of Health: www.nih.gov
United States Postal Service: www.usps.gov
United State Department of Transportation: www.dot.gov
United States Department of Justice: www.usdoj.gov
Security and Exchange Commission: www.sec.gov
Social Security Administration: www.ssa.gov

Nongovernment Agencies:

American Association of Retired Persons (AARP): www.aap.org
Consumer Federation of America (CFA): www.consumerfed.org
Consumers Union: www.consumersunion.org

Consumer World: www.consumerworld.org
Federal Reserve Education: www.federalreserveeducation.org
Identity Theft Resource Center: www.idtheftcenter.org
Internet Scam Busters: www.scambusters.org
National Consumer League: www.ncinet.org
National Foundation for Credit Counseling: www.nfcc.org
National Consumer League's Fraud Center: www.fraud.org

TITHE CHART

Weekly Giving Amount in Dollars
This Chart shows a simple way to grow our giving.

Annual Income	Weekly Income	15%	12%	10%	8%	7%	5%	3%	1%
$ 5,000.00	$ 96.15	$ 14.42	$ 11.54	$ 9.62	$ 7.69	$ 6.73	$ 4.81	$ 2.88	$ 0.96
$ 6,000.00	$ 115.38	$ 17.31	$ 13.85	$ 11.54	$ 9.23	$ 8.08	$ 5.77	$ 3.46	$ 1.15
$ 7,000.00	$ 134.62	$ 20.19	$ 16.15	$ 13.46	$ 10.77	$ 9.42	$ 6.73	$ 4.04	$ 1.35
$ 8,000.00	$ 153.85	$ 23.08	$ 18.46	$ 15.38	$ 12.31	$ 10.77	$ 7.69	$ 4.62	$ 1.54
$ 9,000.00	$ 173.08	$ 25.96	$ 20.77	$ 17.31	$ 13.85	$ 12.12	$ 8.65	$ 5.19	$ 1.73
$ 10,000.00	$ 192.31	$ 28.85	$ 23.08	$ 19.23	$ 15.38	$ 13.46	$ 9.62	$ 5.77	$ 1.92
$ 11,000.00	$ 211.54	$ 31.73	$ 25.38	$ 21.15	$ 16.92	$ 14.81	$ 10.58	$ 6.35	$ 2.12
$ 12,000.00	$ 230.77	$ 34.62	$ 27.69	$ 23.08	$ 18.46	$ 16.15	$ 11.54	$ 6.92	$ 2.31
$ 13,000.00	$ 250.00	$ 37.50	$ 30.00	$ 25.00	$ 20.00	$ 17.50	$ 12.50	$ 7.50	$ 2.50
$ 14,000.00	$ 269.23	$ 40.38	$ 32.31	$ 26.92	$ 21.54	$ 18.85	$ 13.46	$ 8.08	$ 2.69
$ 15,000.00	$ 288.46	$ 43.27	$ 34.62	$ 28.85	$ 23.08	$ 20.19	$ 14.42	$ 8.65	$ 2.88
$ 16,000.00	$ 307.69	$ 46.15	$ 36.92	$ 30.77	$ 24.62	$ 21.54	$ 15.38	$ 9.23	$ 3.08
$ 17,000.00	$ 326.92	$ 49.04	$ 39.23	$ 32.69	$ 26.15	$ 22.88	$ 16.35	$ 9.81	$ 3.27
$ 18,000.00	$ 346.15	$ 51.92	$ 41.54	$ 34.62	$ 27.69	$ 24.23	$ 17.31	$ 10.38	$ 3.46
$ 19,000.00	$ 365.38	$ 54.81	$ 43.85	$ 36.54	$ 29.23	$ 25.58	$ 18.27	$ 10.96	$ 3.65
$ 20,000.00	$ 384.62	$ 57.69	$ 46.15	$ 38.46	$ 30.77	$ 26.92	$ 19.23	$ 11.54	$ 3.85
$ 21,000.00	$ 403.85	$ 60.58	$ 48.46	$ 40.38	$ 32.31	$ 28.27	$ 20.19	$ 12.12	$ 4.04
$ 22,000.00	$ 423.08	$ 63.46	$ 50.77	$ 42.31	$ 33.85	$ 29.62	$ 21.15	$ 12.69	$ 4.23
$ 23,000.00	$ 442.31	$ 66.35	$ 53.08	$ 44.23	$ 35.38	$ 30.96	$ 22.12	$ 13.27	$ 4.42
$ 24,000.00	$ 461.54	$ 69.23	$ 55.38	$ 46.15	$ 36.92	$ 32.31	$ 23.08	$ 13.85	$ 4.62
$ 25,000.00	$ 480.77	$ 72.12	$ 57.69	$ 48.08	$ 38.46	$ 33.65	$ 24.04	$ 14.42	$ 4.81
$ 26,000.00	$ 500.00	$ 75.00	$ 60.00	$ 50.00	$ 40.00	$ 35.00	$ 25.00	$ 15.00	$ 5.00
$ 27,000.00	$ 519.23	$ 77.88	$ 62.31	$ 51.92	$ 41.54	$ 36.35	$ 25.96	$ 15.58	$ 5.19
$ 28,000.00	$ 538.46	$ 80.77	$ 64.62	$ 53.85	$ 43.08	$ 37.69	$ 26.92	$ 16.15	$ 5.38
$ 29,000.00	$ 557.69	$ 83.65	$ 66.92	$ 55.77	$ 44.62	$ 39.04	$ 27.88	$ 16.73	$ 5.58
$ 30,000.00	$ 576.92	$ 86.54	$ 69.23	$ 57.69	$ 46.15	$ 40.38	$ 28.85	$ 17.31	$ 5.77
$ 31,000.00	$ 596.15	$ 89.42	$ 71.54	$ 59.62	$ 47.69	$ 41.73	$ 29.81	$ 17.88	$ 5.96
$ 32,000.00	$ 615.38	$ 92.31	$ 73.85	$ 61.54	$ 49.23	$ 43.08	$ 30.77	$ 18.46	$ 6.15
$ 33,000.00	$ 634.62	$ 95.19	$ 76.15	$ 63.46	$ 50.77	$ 44.42	$ 31.73	$ 19.04	$ 6.35
$ 34,000.00	$ 653.85	$ 98.08	$ 78.46	$ 65.38	$ 52.31	$ 45.77	$ 32.69	$ 19.62	$ 6.54
$ 35,000.00	$ 673.08	$ 100.96	$ 80.77	$ 67.31	$ 53.85	$ 47.12	$ 33.65	$ 20.19	$ 6.73
$ 36,000.00	$ 692.31	$ 103.85	$ 83.08	$ 69.23	$ 55.38	$ 48.46	$ 34.62	$ 20.77	$ 6.92
$ 37,000.00	$ 711.54	$ 106.73	$ 85.38	$ 71.15	$ 56.92	$ 49.81	$ 35.58	$ 21.35	$ 7.12
$ 38,000.00	$ 730.77	$ 109.62	$ 87.69	$ 73.08	$ 58.46	$ 51.15	$ 36.54	$ 21.92	$ 7.31
$ 39,000.00	$ 750.00	$ 112.50	$ 90.00	$ 75.00	$ 60.00	$ 52.50	$ 37.50	$ 22.50	$ 7.50
$ 40,000.00	$ 769.23	$ 115.38	$ 92.31	$ 76.92	$ 61.54	$ 53.85	$ 38.46	$ 23.08	$ 7.69
$ 41,000.00	$ 788.46	$ 118.27	$ 94.62	$ 78.85	$ 63.08	$ 55.19	$ 39.42	$ 23.65	$ 7.88
$ 42,000.00	$ 807.69	$ 121.15	$ 96.92	$ 80.77	$ 64.62	$ 56.54	$ 40.38	$ 24.23	$ 8.08
$ 43,000.00	$ 826.92	$ 124.04	$ 99.23	$ 82.69	$ 66.15	$ 57.88	$ 41.35	$ 24.81	$ 8.27
$ 44,000.00	$ 846.15	$ 126.92	$ 101.54	$ 84.62	$ 67.69	$ 59.23	$ 42.31	$ 25.38	$ 8.46
$ 45,000.00	$ 865.38	$ 129.81	$ 103.85	$ 86.54	$ 69.23	$ 60.58	$ 43.27	$ 25.96	$ 8.65
$ 46,000.00	$ 884.62	$ 132.69	$ 106.15	$ 88.46	$ 70.77	$ 61.92	$ 44.23	$ 26.54	$ 8.85
$ 47,000.00	$ 903.85	$ 135.58	$ 108.46	$ 90.38	$ 72.31	$ 63.27	$ 45.19	$ 27.12	$ 9.04
$ 48,000.00	$ 923.08	$ 138.46	$ 110.77	$ 92.31	$ 73.85	$ 64.62	$ 46.15	$ 27.69	$ 9.23
$ 49,000.00	$ 942.31	$ 141.35	$ 113.08	$ 94.23	$ 75.38	$ 65.96	$ 47.12	$ 28.27	$ 9.42
$ 50,000.00	$ 961.54	$ 144.23	$ 115.38	$ 96.15	$ 76.92	$ 67.31	$ 48.08	$ 28.85	$ 9.62
$ 51,000.00	$ 980.77	$ 147.12	$ 117.69	$ 98.08	$ 78.46	$ 68.65	$ 49.04	$ 29.42	$ 9.81
$ 52,000.00	$1,000.00	$ 150.00	$ 120.00	$ 100.00	$ 80.00	$ 70.00	$ 50.00	$ 30.00	$ 10.00
$ 53,000.00	$1,019.23	$ 152.88	$ 122.31	$ 101.92	$ 81.54	$ 71.35	$ 50.96	$ 30.58	$ 10.19
$ 54,000.00	$1,038.46	$ 155.77	$ 124.62	$ 103.85	$ 83.08	$ 72.69	$ 51.92	$ 31.15	$ 10.38

Annual Income	Weekly Income	15%	12%	10%	8%	7%	5%	3%	1%
$ 55,000.00	$1,057.69	$ 158.65	$ 126.92	$ 105.77	$ 84.62	$ 74.04	$ 52.88	$ 31.73	$ 10.58
$ 56,000.00	$1,076.92	$ 161.54	$ 129.23	$ 107.69	$ 86.15	$ 75.38	$ 53.85	$ 32.31	$ 10.77
$ 57,000.00	$1,096.15	$ 164.42	$ 131.54	$ 109.62	$ 87.69	$ 76.73	$ 54.81	$ 32.88	$ 10.96
$ 58,000.00	$1,115.38	$ 167.31	$ 133.85	$ 111.54	$ 89.23	$ 78.08	$ 55.77	$ 33.46	$ 11.15
$ 59,000.00	$1,134.62	$ 170.19	$ 136.15	$ 113.46	$ 90.77	$ 79.42	$ 56.73	$ 34.04	$ 11.35
$ 60,000.00	$1,153.85	$ 173.08	$ 138.46	$ 115.38	$ 92.31	$ 80.77	$ 57.69	$ 34.62	$ 11.54
$ 61,000.00	$1,173.08	$ 175.96	$ 140.77	$ 117.31	$ 93.85	$ 82.12	$ 58.65	$ 35.19	$ 11.73
$ 62,000.00	$1,192.31	$ 178.85	$ 143.08	$ 119.23	$ 95.38	$ 83.46	$ 59.62	$ 35.77	$ 11.92
$ 63,000.00	$1,211.54	$ 181.73	$ 145.38	$ 121.15	$ 96.92	$ 84.81	$ 60.58	$ 36.35	$ 12.12
$ 64,000.00	$1,230.77	$ 184.62	$ 147.69	$ 123.08	$ 98.46	$ 86.15	$ 61.54	$ 36.92	$ 12.31
$ 65,000.00	$1,250.00	$ 187.50	$ 150.00	$ 125.00	$ 100.00	$ 87.50	$ 62.50	$ 37.50	$ 12.50
$ 66,000.00	$1,269.23	$ 190.38	$ 152.31	$ 126.92	$ 101.54	$ 88.85	$ 63.46	$ 38.08	$ 12.69
$ 67,000.00	$1,288.46	$ 193.27	$ 154.62	$ 128.85	$ 103.08	$ 90.19	$ 64.42	$ 38.65	$ 12.88
$ 68,000.00	$1,307.69	$ 196.15	$ 156.92	$ 130.77	$ 104.62	$ 91.54	$ 65.38	$ 39.23	$ 13.08
$ 69,000.00	$1,326.92	$ 199.04	$ 159.23	$ 132.69	$ 106.15	$ 92.88	$ 66.35	$ 39.81	$ 13.27
$ 70,000.00	$1,346.15	$ 201.92	$ 161.54	$ 134.62	$ 107.69	$ 94.23	$ 67.31	$ 40.38	$ 13.46
$ 71,000.00	$1,365.38	$ 204.81	$ 163.85	$ 136.54	$ 109.23	$ 95.58	$ 68.27	$ 40.96	$ 13.65
$ 72,000.00	$1,384.62	$ 207.69	$ 166.15	$ 138.46	$ 110.77	$ 96.92	$ 69.23	$ 41.54	$ 13.85
$ 73,000.00	$1,403.85	$ 210.58	$ 168.46	$ 140.38	$ 112.31	$ 98.27	$ 70.19	$ 42.12	$ 14.04
$ 74,000.00	$1,423.08	$ 213.46	$ 170.77	$ 142.31	$ 113.85	$ 99.62	$ 71.15	$ 42.69	$ 14.23
$ 75,000.00	$1,442.31	$ 216.35	$ 173.08	$ 144.23	$ 115.38	$ 100.96	$ 72.12	$ 43.27	$ 14.42
$ 76,000.00	$1,461.54	$ 219.23	$ 175.38	$ 146.15	$ 116.92	$ 102.31	$ 73.08	$ 43.85	$ 14.62
$ 77,000.00	$1,480.77	$ 222.12	$ 177.69	$ 148.08	$ 118.46	$ 103.65	$ 74.04	$ 44.42	$ 14.81
$ 78,000.00	$1,500.00	$ 225.00	$ 180.00	$ 150.00	$ 120.00	$ 105.00	$ 75.00	$ 45.00	$ 15.00
$ 79,000.00	$1,519.23	$ 227.88	$ 182.31	$ 151.92	$ 121.54	$ 106.35	$ 75.96	$ 45.58	$ 15.19
$ 80,000.00	$1,538.46	$ 230.77	$ 184.62	$ 153.85	$ 123.08	$ 107.69	$ 76.92	$ 46.15	$ 15.38
$ 81,000.00	$1,557.69	$ 233.65	$ 186.92	$ 155.77	$ 124.62	$ 109.04	$ 77.88	$ 46.73	$ 15.58
$ 82,000.00	$1,576.92	$ 236.54	$ 189.23	$ 157.69	$ 126.15	$ 110.38	$ 78.85	$ 47.31	$ 15.77
$ 83,000.00	$1,596.15	$ 239.42	$ 191.54	$ 159.62	$ 127.69	$ 111.73	$ 79.81	$ 47.88	$ 15.96
$ 84,000.00	$1,615.38	$ 242.31	$ 193.85	$ 161.54	$ 129.23	$ 113.08	$ 80.77	$ 48.46	$ 16.15
$ 85,000.00	$1,634.62	$ 245.19	$ 196.15	$ 163.46	$ 130.77	$ 114.42	$ 81.73	$ 49.04	$ 16.35
$ 86,000.00	$1,653.85	$ 248.08	$ 198.46	$ 165.38	$ 132.31	$ 115.77	$ 82.69	$ 49.62	$ 16.54
$ 87,000.00	$1,673.08	$ 250.96	$ 200.77	$ 167.31	$ 133.85	$ 117.12	$ 83.65	$ 50.19	$ 16.73
$ 88,000.00	$1,692.31	$ 253.85	$ 203.08	$ 169.23	$ 135.38	$ 118.46	$ 84.62	$ 50.77	$ 16.92
$ 89,000.00	$1,711.54	$ 256.73	$ 205.38	$ 171.15	$ 136.92	$ 119.81	$ 85.58	$ 51.35	$ 17.12
$ 90,000.00	$1,730.77	$ 259.62	$ 207.69	$ 173.08	$ 138.46	$ 121.15	$ 86.54	$ 51.92	$ 17.31
$ 91,000.00	$1,750.00	$ 262.50	$ 210.00	$ 175.00	$ 140.00	$ 122.50	$ 87.50	$ 52.50	$ 17.50
$ 92,000.00	$1,769.23	$ 265.38	$ 212.31	$ 176.92	$ 141.54	$ 123.85	$ 88.46	$ 53.08	$ 17.69
$ 93,000.00	$1,788.46	$ 268.27	$ 214.62	$ 178.85	$ 143.08	$ 125.19	$ 89.42	$ 53.65	$ 17.88
$ 94,000.00	$1,807.69	$ 271.15	$ 216.92	$ 180.77	$ 144.62	$ 126.54	$ 90.38	$ 54.23	$ 18.08
$ 95,000.00	$1,826.92	$ 274.04	$ 219.23	$ 182.69	$ 146.15	$ 127.88	$ 91.35	$ 54.81	$ 18.27
$ 96,000.00	$1,846.15	$ 276.92	$ 221.54	$ 184.62	$ 147.69	$ 129.23	$ 92.31	$ 55.38	$ 18.46
$ 97,000.00	$1,865.38	$ 279.81	$ 223.85	$ 186.54	$ 149.23	$ 130.58	$ 93.27	$ 55.96	$ 18.65
$ 98,000.00	$1,884.62	$ 282.69	$ 226.15	$ 188.46	$ 150.77	$ 131.92	$ 94.23	$ 56.54	$ 18.85
$ 99,000.00	$1,903.85	$ 285.58	$ 228.46	$ 190.38	$ 152.31	$ 133.27	$ 95.19	$ 57.12	$ 19.04
$100,000.00	$1,923.08	$ 288.46	$ 230.77	$ 192.31	$ 153.85	$ 134.62	$ 96.15	$ 57.69	$ 19.23

Calculate your current weekly giving amount.

My Current Giving is: $_____ = _____%

My Goal is to increase my giving to: $_____ = _____%
**A challenge is to increase your giving.

DEBT STACKING METHOD

List of Debt	Balance	Interest Rate	Monthly Payment	Old Balance	New payment	New Balance	Put in Number Order by Highest Interest Rate

Debt Stacking is paying off the cards with the highest interest rates first, while making the minimum payments on the others.

DEBT-TO-INCOME RATIO CALCULATOR

This form is intended to help calculate your debt to income ratio. List your monthly income in the appropriate boxes. Be sure to include ALL income and ALL monthly debt payments for accurate results. To get a general idea of what type of home you can afford, multiply your annual gross income (before taxes) by 3. For example, if your annual household income is $50,000, you might be able to qualify for a $150,000 home.

Monthly Income (Take Home)	
Salary / Wages 1	
Salary / Wages 2	
Other Income	
Total Income	

Debt to Income Ratio (Calculated)	
Monthly Debt Payment	
(divided by)	
Monthly Income	
(Equals)	
Debt to Income Ratio	

Total Monthly Debt Payments	
Monthy mortgage payments	
Credit Card payments	
Student Loans	
Car Payments	
Bank/ Credit Union/Loan payments	
Medical Dental Bill Payments	
Computer / Electronic Bill Payments	
Furniture and Appliance Payments	
Other Credit Loans or Accounts	
Total Monthly Income	

The following is how creditors rate your DTI:

less than 10%	Great Credit
10-20%	Good Credit
20-35%	Low Credit Risk
35% or Higher	High Credit Risk

MONTHLY INCOME ALLOCATION (MIA) CALCULATION

	<<Enter Net Pay
	10% Tithe
	10% Savings Account
	25% Rent or mortgage
	10% Utilities (water, sewer, natural gas, electric)
	10% Groceries
	10% Car loan or lease payments and/or public transportation, fuel
	10% Debt repayment (credit cards, revolving charge accounts, personal loans, student loans)
	5% Clothes, shoes, accessories, etc.
	5% Entertainment, including eating out
	5% Vehicle (insurance premium, vehicle registration fee, driver's license renewal, etc.)

Use the percentages for your household budget to plan how you will spend your paycheck each month.

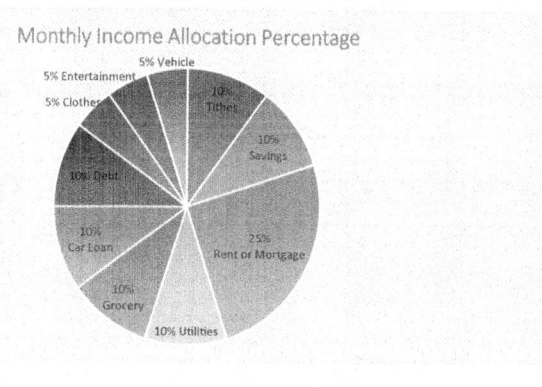

Monthly Income Allocation Percentage

- 5% Vehicle
- 10% Tithes
- 10% Savings
- 25% Rent or Mortgage
- 10% Utilities
- 10% Grocery
- 10% Car Loan
- 10% Debt
- 5% Clothes
- 5% Entertainment

MONTHLY BUDGET TEMPLATE

Household Income	Week 1	Week 2	Week 3	Week 4	Week 5	Total
Household Income 1						$ -
Household Income 2						$ -
Other Income						$ -
Total Household Income	$ -	$ -	$ -	$ -	$ -	$ -
Household Expense	Week 1	Week 2	Week 3	Week 4	Week 5	Total
Tithes						$ -
Savings Account						$ -
Housing (Rent/Mortgage)						$ -
Electricity						$ -
Water/Gas						$ -
Home Phone						$ -
Cell Phone						$ -
Computer Online-Service						$ -
Cable						$ -
Food						$ -
Car Payments						$ -
Gas / Oil						$ -
Toll Tag						$ -
Medical / Dental						$ -
Childcare						$ -
Household items						$ -
Personal Items						$ -
Credit Cards						$ -
Loans						$ -
Other Expense						$ -
Total Household Expenses	$ -	$ -	$ -	$ -	$ -	$ -
Household Income (Loss)	$0.00	$0.00	$0.00	$0.00	$0.00	$0.00

Note:
1. Add up all of your weekly/monthly household income to get your total household income
2. Add up all of your weekly/monthly expenses to get your total household expenses
3. Subtract your total household expenses from your total household income to get your available household income

    Example:
        Total Income: $ 1,500.00
        Total Expenses: $ 650.00
        Net Income: $ 850.00 <<< Available Income

NET WORTH STATEMENT

ASSETS	
Cash on Hand	$
Cash in Checking	$
Cash in Savings Account	$
Money Market Accounts	$
Market Value of Your Home	$
Estimated Value of Household Items	$
Market Value of Other Real Estate	$
Stocks	$
Bonds	$
Mutual Funds	$
Market Value of Vehicles	$
Cash Value of Life Insurance	$
Current Value of 401K plan or similar retirement Account	$
Individual Retirement Account (IRA, Roth IRA)	$
Estimated Value of Personal Items (including collectables)	$
Other Assets	$
TOTAL ASSETS	$

LIABILITIES (List the remaining balances)	
Mortgage	$
Home Equity Loan or Line of Credit	$
Other Real Estate Loans	$
Auto Loan or Lease	$
Credit Card Balances	$
Student Loans	$
Delinquent Taxes	$
401 K Loan	$
Personal Unsecured Loans	$
Life Insurance Loans	$
Other Liabilities	$
TOTAL LIABILITIES	$

NET WORTH	$

Note:
1. Add up all of your assets to get your total assets
2. Add up all of your liabilities to get your total liabilities
3. Subtract your total liabilities from your total assets to get your net worth

Example:
Total Assets: $ 25,000.00
Total Liabilities $ 15,500.00
Net Worth >>> $ 9,500.00

CREDITOR SETTLEMENT AGREEMENT LETTER

Date

Name of Collection Agency
Address
City, ST Zip Code

Re: **Credit Settle Agreement; Account of [name account is under]; Account No. [insert account number]**

To Whom It May Concern:

I am experiencing a financial hardship due to _____. As a result, I am unable to repay this debt in full. I am writing to ask if you would be willing to accept half of the amount owed as payment in full. If you agree to accept half, I can send you a cashier's check [or money order] as soon as I receive notice that you will accept my offer.

If you agree to these terms, please sign and date this letter and return it to me. After receiving it, I will send you a check in the amount of $_____, which will constitute payment in full and release me from all further collection efforts by both the original creditor and your collection agency.

Accepted and Agreed

By: _____

Name: _____

Title: _____

Sincerely,

Your Name

NOTES

Introduction

1. Strauss, Richard. 1985. *Getting Along With Each Other*. San Bernadino: Here's Life Publisher.
2. Rebecca Lake, "Lottery Winner Statistics: 23 Eye-Popping Facts" https://www.creditdonkey.com/lottery-winner-statistics.html
3. Mankiw, Gregory N. 1998. *Principles of Economics*. Orlando: Harcourt Brace College Publishers.

Day 1: A New Covenant with God

1. Hiscox, Michael D, Vicki L Spandel, and Mary L Lewis. 2004. "Business And The Law." In *Business And The Law*, by Michael D Hiscox, Vicki L Spandel and Mary L Lewis, 65. Pasadena: Thomas South-Western West.

Day 2: Under New Management

1. 2001. In *Business In Action*, by Courtland L Bovee and John V Thill, 134. Upper Saddle River: Pearson Prentice Hall.

Day 3: First Fruits

1. Associates for Scriptural Knowledge. 2014. *The Mosaic Law of Tithing*. http://www.askelm.com/tithing/thi006.htm.

Day 4: Write the Vision

1. 2001. In *Business In Action*, by Courtland L Bovee and John V Thill, 134. Upper Saddle River: Pearson Prentice Hall.
2. Robbins, Stephen P. 2016. Chapter 9. Supervision Today! Boston: Pearson.

Day 5: Financial Equality

1. Drew DeSilver, "5 Facts about Economic Inequality," Pew Research Center RSS, 2014, http://www.pewresearch.org/fact-tank/2014/01/07/5-facts- about-economic-inequality/.

Day 6: God's Power to Do More

1. Campbell, Sally R. 2010. *Foundations of Personal Finance 8th Edition*. Tinley Park: The Goodheart-Willcox Company, Inc.

Day 9: Serving a Miracle-Working God

1. Hiscox, Michael D, Vicki L Spandel, and Mary L Lewis. 2004. "Business And The Law." In *Business And The Law*, by Michael D Hiscox, Vicki L Spandel and Mary L Lewis, 65. Pasadena: Thomas South-Western West.

Day 10: Breaking the Financial Curse

1. Gondwe, Eric. 2008. *Chapter 7. Christian Deliverance and Healing in Financial Health Areas*. http://www.spiritualwarfaredeliverance.com/html/deliverance-and-healing-06.html.

Day 11: Putting Faith in Action

1. 2017. *Salary Genius: Methodist Pastor Salary in Texas*. http://salarygenius.com/tx/dallas/salary/methodist-pastor-salary.

Day 13: Being Content

1. 2017. Nielsen: http://www.nielsen.com/us/en/about-us.html.

Day 16: Being a Generous Giver

1. 2013. Lane Southern Orchards. http://www.lanesouthernorchards.com/about-us.

Day 18: Investing Wisely

1. National Association of Investors Corporation. 2001. Investing in Your Future. 34-35. Mason: South-Western.

CPSIA information can be obtained
at www.ICGtesting.com
Printed in the USA
BVOW08s0725250617
487770BV00001B/67/P

9 781512 783735